Positively Productive

Positively Productive

Kelly Cookson

authors
AND CO.

First published in Great Britain in 2023
by Authors & Co.
www.authorsandco.pub

ISBN 978-1-915771-30-8 (paperback)

Medical Disclaimer

This book contains general information about medications and treatments. The information is not advice, and should not be treated as such. Do not substitute this information for the medical advice of physicians. The information contained in this book is based on the personal and professional experiences of the author. Always consult your doctor for yours and your family's individual needs.

Contents

Introduction

Chances are you've picked up this book because you're looking for a way to bend time and space to get everything done in your life and business. I get it! You've seen plenty of entrepreneurs juggle work and family life to create insanely successful businesses and you want a piece of that action.

You're willing to dig down, do the work and build the business of your dreams. If you could just figure out HOW to get everything done in time to hit your next goal...

If you're a parent like me, you'll likely be familiar with trying to dodge unexpected curveballs that life throws at you, derailing your plans to crack on with that big project which is going to take your business to the next level. As I write this in early 2023, we've had school strikes and sick bugs galore. Penny also decided it was time to become scared of the dark! I've had quite a few sleep-deprived nights and days at work where I've only been able to get the bare minimum done.

Even when you're not a parent, life still gives you plenty of admin headaches and time-sucking challenges to overcome. I've lost count of how many times I've taken my car to the garage this year!

The problem with having to change your plans at the last minute is that it creates overwhelm. You can feel time slipping away and there's a real fear that you'll get to the end of the year and realise you're no further forward with your business or that lifestyle you dream of creating.

Maybe you're constantly chasing your tail and it's all that you can do to tackle the 'must do' tasks in your business such as show up for your clients, pay the bills, or reply to all those emails that have been piling up. There's no time or head-space to work ON your business when you're stuck working IN it.

When there's financial pressure on top of your never-ending to do list, you can feel like you're treading water and maybe you are stuck doing work that you don't like - just to pay the bills.

That dream you had when you started your business seems unachievable at this point. You'd imagined having MORE time to be with your kids or pursue your interests outside of work, but in reality, you're cramming work into any spare pocket of time you have, so it feels like you're never switching off. What happened to having fun? Taking random days off midweek to swan around the shops with the retired folk while everyone else is grinding it out at work? Maybe you dreamed of having more time to visit family or take mini breaks with your partner or best friend. You've realised that instead of being the master of your time, your business has total control over you. This means that you feel stressed, or snappy and sometimes you might even consider jacking it all in and applying for a job as a supermarket shelf stacker. Don't do that! There *is* enough time in your week to make real progress towards your goals; to fill your cup, to be a present parent, a good friend, fun partner AND build a successful business - I'm proof of that.

Despite all the time I've lost so far this year dodging curveballs and dealing with life admin, I've managed to have the most financially successful start to the year in my business yet. I've found the time to write this book and begin to learn how to play the guitar. I've been to the spa with my bestie and treated my family to a weekend away where I left my phone switched off. How have I found the time and creative head-space to do that? That's what I'm about to share with you. You can do this too.

This book is going to give you permission to enjoy your life right NOW. I'm not going to let you wait until your business is a "success" to start living the life you want. I'm not talking about living beyond your means financially - I'm talking about taking time out for yourself every day because if you can't do that now, you won't do it when your business is bringing in more money.

The better you feel, the more successful you will be in business. I have a mantra (which folks must be sick of seeing all over my Instagram stories with a selfie of me in my gym gear, but it works so I'll share it here): "The more I go to the gym, the more money I make."

I'm not going to tell you to go to the gym if that's your idea of hell - but I am going to tell you to insert your version of "the gym" in a mantra of your very own.

Don't worry - this isn't a money manifestation book! There are plenty of those out there and feel free to

DM me if you want to know my favourites. Instead, this book is about increasing your motivation and productivity using scientifically proven tools to help you feel more engaged with and excited about your work. I'm going to share some powerful 'Positive Psychology' interventions with you which will help you to shift from time scarcity, fear of failure and overwhelm into confidence, flow and an entrepreneurial spirit that will never be crushed. Get ready!

Alongside Positive Psychology to boost your performance, I'm sharing the time management strategies that I've developed after meticulously tracking my own time and finding out where it was draining away. I'm not regurgitating the tactics that 'middle-aged white dudes' tout in the usual time management books. They don't have kids to take care of for a start and as far as I can tell, they aren't interested in making it to a Friday morning yoga class and sauna session. I've got time management hacks that WORK for business owners who don't have a big team around them and that have other commitments such as kids, needy cats, elderly parents, a neglected partner, health goals and pursuits outside of work, work work.

We're also going to look at your content marketing strategy (or lack of!) because there are changes you can make to improve how efficiently and consistently you market your business. I have a business degree where I specialised in marketing and at the time of writing this, fifteen years' experience working in marketing.

I took my secret side hustle as a freelance marketer to my main gig and a six-figure turnover just two and a half years after I left my job as a marketing manager. I left that safe, corporate job at the end of 2019 and, of course, you know what happened just three months into going full-time with my fledgling business - the COVID-19 pandemic. Thanks to lockdown I was suddenly tasked with having my three-year-old at home whilst keeping up with client work and my own marketing so the business could keep going. This wasn't what I had signed up for! My husband Adam's job meant he continued to go to work everyday and he would take over parenting when he got home while I worked. Trying to focus on client work at 5 p.m. after wrangling a toddler around all day was not the vibe I was looking for but the work had to get done. It was tough and I totally broke down mid-May with the weight of it all and sheer frustration (as many of us did) but I'm proud to say that I consistently grew my business thanks to the smart marketing strategy I stuck to and a big mindset shift that summer. If I can market and grow a business in a pandemic whilst potty-training a toddler - I can do anything! At the very least, I can show you how to become more efficient in your business and get more of the important stuff done so you can see some progress.

To build a reliable income stream and get into a rhythm of running your business you need to be consistent with your marketing. We've got to address what the hell you're doing with Social Media and I'm going to push you to make some big changes to your content marketing. If you're reading this and you can't remember the last time you actually did some marketing for your business - great! I'm going to show you a new way to get in front of your ideal clients that doesn't take hours of your time.

I reached that six-figure turnover milestone working just twenty hours a week and if I can find time to market my business successfully alongside serving my clients and creating new offers and services then you can.

Here's the magic of the culmination of everything I'm sharing with you in this book; you're going to enjoy your life and business more right away. You can stop waiting to hit that financial goal or have more spare time to do the stuff that makes you feel good.

By adopting my approach and changing your focus from 'busy work' to the tasks that make a real difference to where you want to take your business– you will be back in control. You started your business for a reason and I can assure you that you're not alone in having created a beast that seems to have a life of its own. The good news is that you can absolutely change gear and start to reap the rewards of being your own boss. You're about to take back the power. Pause for a moment to imagine how that will feel.

If you're not sure that this will work for you, and you're doubting it's possible to feel great about your business and enjoy the process right now (before you hit that milestone you've set where you'll deem your business a success), I'd like to share some examples of the impact my mentoring across marketing strategy, time management and positive mindset has had on my clients.

Like the story of my client who went from struggling to pay the bills in her PR business to having her highest revenue month ever by signing new retainer clients to secure her baseline income. We used Positive Psychology to focus on how she could feel happier and enjoy her life right now - instead of striving to make money. By improving my client's outlook for her life and business she began to attract new clients and find the time and motivation to create other revenue streams. This was all achieved working school hours.

Or the single mum of two who was paralysed by overwhelm and felt like her copywriting business was in control of her, rather than the other way around. The time-saving methods I shared were so powerful and simple that they could be implemented straight away and had an immediate impact. My client went on to secure new business and create the head-space to work on the projects to grow her business.

Then there's me! I'm an example of what can happen when you get focussed on the right things, give yourself time to restore, look after your own well-being and connect with WHY you're in business at all. It was when I started to get clarity on what I really wanted that my business took off.

Hopefully you're now feeling fired up to discover all the Positively Productive strategies I'm about to share with you. This book is designed to give you practical advice so I recommend bookmarking the pages where you have your lightbulb moments and taking this book to work with you so you can start to implement what you've learned straight away.

Let's get started!

Chapter 1

Dreaming bigger

I didn't set out with an ambitious money goal for my business. When I started moonlighting as a freelance marketer on the side of my day job I used the extra cash to pay towards treats like our summer holiday or family days out. The money was a welcome bonus on the side of my part-time marketing manager salary and I never planned that the side hustle money would evolve to become my sole income just nine months later.

I had no intention of leaving my marketing manager job to work for myself. In fact, it was safe to say, I was the anti-entrepreneur. I saw entrepreneurs as a different breed. People in power suits who raised capital and pitched to investors and grew Million Dollar Companies. The Apprentice and Dragons' Den may be partly to blame for this perception. Entrepreneurs seemed totally alien to me as a normal person. My family were bus drivers! We didn't start companies. I think this is important for you to know right at the outset, because before I started my business I presumed that I lacked entrepreneurial acumen and it just goes to show that this can change and if *I* can build a six-figure business, so can you! I still don't own a power suit by the way...

My first exposure to real-life entrepreneurship, a far cry from what I had seen on the TV, was watching other people work really hard to start a business based on their exciting idea and failing to make it succeed long term. I used to work at The University of Nottingham in the Institute for Innovation and Entrepreneurship and I saw first-hand how young entrepreneurs struggled to get their fledgling businesses off the ground. The ones that did well seemed mature beyond their years and so confident! They were attending a red brick university after all, and I imagined they came from wealthy families with parents, aunts, uncles and siblings who had all gone to university before them. Then there were the local SMEs who came to the university looking for support to grow, they seemed to eat, sleep and dream about their businesses. It all looked very time-consuming, tiring and risky because it was all on them to succeed and pay themselves and their team. In contrast, my employment at the university was very cushy where I could take leisurely two-hour lunches to stroll around campus and find a pleasant spot to read my book. I got all of my work done and more so there were no complaints from my colleagues and I was happy coasting along, taking my pay increase each year and enjoying the Business School summer BBQs.

I was happy until I inevitably got bored. I was sitting at my desk one day and realised I could easily work at the university until retirement. I saw decades slip by in a blur of the same faces, staff socials and long meetings. My colleagues were lovely, my office was in a state-of-the-art, space age building. I had an ergonomic chair and we were treated to yoga classes and mindfulness during work time. Friday mornings were allocated to networking with free coffee and cakes and university catering was pretty good. I got to watch expert guest speakers like Karren Brady give inspiring talks (but entrepreneurship was still not for me) and eat up all the university canapés I could stomach. I still miss the cream teas... Life was good.

But I started to get an itch and questioned if I really wanted to become completely institutionalised and give up ever going back to corporate. I decided to keep my eyes open for marketing opportunities that might excite me a little more.

I'm a big believer in walking through doors that open for you, or at least giving the handle a little jiggle and peeping through to see what might be on the other side. I did this with various job adverts until I got excited enough about a post to apply for it and ended up receiving an offer. I think in the interview I clinched it when I was asked what my favourite music is and I replied with Deftones (heavy metal) and Beyonce. I also did a presentation to the CEO composed entirely out of emoji. Nailed it! I decided to take the offer and when I told my university boss. he wished me well and predicted that when I had a taste of corporate again, I wouldn't want to come back to higher education.

My new employer was an agile, young(ish) tech company and from day two I wore my trainers to work and officially retired my smart pencil skirts and shift dresses. Day one I made the mistake of turning up to my desk in my university work attire and I stuck out like a sore thumb.

I'll fast forward through the next two years because nothing major happened until I got pregnant and had my daughter, Penny, in April 2017. My pregnancy was fairly uneventful with the exception of gestational diabetes which coincided with Easter (cruel) and I went off on maternity leave to return part-time when Penny was nine months old. I was ready to go back to work and enjoy eating my lunch without being interrupted and it was nice to engage my brain again. I was grateful to have the support from my boss at the time – a six foot plus rugby coaching CEO who facilitated my ability to train our marketing assistant to take on aspects of my role so I could return to work for three days a week instead of full time. It was a really positive experience for me and, of course, some days I had a little weep in the car when I left Penny at nursery if she cried for me; but overall we were both fine with our new routine. On the days when I wasn't particularly engaged with the project I was working on and Penny had been dropped at nursery with a cold, or was reaching for me as I handed her over, I think the seed planted in my mind that I might want to jack it all in and have more time with her.

After two years of working three-day weeks, an ex-colleague from my university days got in touch to ask if I'd do a bit of marketing for her on the side - paid of course. I said "yes" and found that I really enjoyed working on marketing that wasn't about software. I also enjoyed the little boost it gave to my bank balance.

Here I was making some money on the side doing small marketing projects and I started to wonder how much work I could fit in during nap times and my evenings to earn even more. I loved listening to podcasts on the commute to work to get some ideas on how to scale the good thing I had going on alongside the day job. I started listening to shows like The Freelance Fix and Side Hustle School. I was open to ideas about how I might run my side gig and lean into where I might want to take it.

A few dozen hours of podcasts later, I started to feel excited about the potential of my freelancing. Excitement is one of the first cues I want you to become aware of when it comes to your life and business. When you get that fluttery feeling of new possibilities and you can see a chance to do something that feels invigorating and it starts to light you up and you think about it all the time - don't swat away or squash that feeling! That excited feeling was the first indication that I should start my own business properly. I've noticed that feeling with every pivot and radical change I've made along the way since I went all in with the business and it's never done me wrong. It's called intuition and listening to yours is one of the more important signposts on the journey of creating a business and a lifestyle that you love.

If you're from a corporate background like I am then you've probably never been told to listen to your gut. Employment taught me how to make decisions based on ROI, team resources and deadlines. Personal development at work consisted of training courses on how to use new software and a little bit on team management. As a middle manager, I missed out on the DISC assessments the directors had as part of their personal development. I guess there wasn't the budget to extend coaching to the wider team. Back then, I didn't even know that business coaching was a thing. If you'd asked me what a coach did, I would've said coaches were for athletes. Coaching and mentorship is an essential part of my life now.

So there I was. In my car on the way to work, sometimes in a traffic jam, sometimes shedding a tear because Penny had cried when I dropped her off at nursery and I was listening to podcast interviews with people making a killing with their side hustle. I vividly remember one woman reported bringing in $6000 a month drawing pet portraits! I started to dream bigger than staying in my safe job and settling for my meagre, pro-rated salary.

Just one year later I had left my job and I was officially an entrepreneur.

Building a monster

The first six months of running my business were intense. Thanks to side-hustling and reaching out to my network, I had built a small roster of clients and landed a new retainer straight out of the gate. I also sold my services back to my former employer and negotiated a retainer to continue some of the copywriting work I had been doing. That was a sweaty moment for me in my boss's office negotiating an hourly rate with a guy renowned for driving a hard bargain. I did it because I was so fired up about making my business work and I had a strict financial goal to match my salary immediately. That minimum monthly revenue was a target I wouldn't miss and I'm proud that I backed myself to secure that income.

I'd left my job at the end of December 2019 and come 1st January 2020 it was all on me to make the money to pay myself. I had reduced Penny's childcare from three long days at the nursery near my old office to around sixteen hours at a preschool closer to home. We were spending more time together and I was happy that she was happy. This was our routine for the first ten weeks of my self-employed life, this was our routine. I was having to figure out all the stuff that comes with running a business; invoicing, saving for tax, other admin tasks and I was working extra hours when Penny went to bed to make sure that I had everything covered. But life was good. I was making the money I needed all by myself - go me!

Then from 23rd March 2020 we were in lockdown. Preschool was closed and I was faced with running my business stuck in our house with a toddler in tow. It was a really testing time for me because I keenly felt the stress from the pile of client work waiting for me and almost no time other than if I could get Penny to have a midday nap to get it done. I had to work an hour before dawn and squeeze the rest in from late afternoon when Adam got home from work and could take over parenting. This was not the vision I'd had for my newly self-employed life! I didn't lose any clients during the pandemic - they all recognised they needed to keep marketing their way through the situation to be ready for coming out of lockdown. So there wasn't any financial stress, but the mental side of not really being in control of my work schedule and having to turn on the creative juices after being mum all day was exhausting.

When things finally started to move towards 'the new normal' I was left with a feeling that I'd created a business I didn't truly love. I had a lot of clients (great!) but I was grossly undercharging so to make sure I hit my financial target, I said "yes" to any project that came along, whether I wanted to do the work or not. In fact, I never considered turning down paid work. I kept adding to my plate and never thought about when I would find the time to do the work. I said "yes" and got on with it. This is what I thought growing a business was all about. Doing more. I stole hours from my free time to work on client projects. I worked later into the evening and I set Penny up with games to play while I worked alongside her. I got the work done but I started to resent it.

Then I had a chance meeting with someone who would open my mind to doing things differently. My path crossed with an Intuitive Coach and at that time I had no idea what that was. I'd been asked to give some feedback on her website design and when I started to read about her coaching services for entrepreneurs like me I was amazed that this was even a thing! This wasn't personal development that I recognised. It was about listening to your heart and opening your mind. I was intrigued. Did people really pay for this? And did it really help? Couldn't I just open my heart and mind by myself? Where would I even start with that?

As the coach and I chatted, one thing led to another and I found myself sitting at her kitchen table creating a vision board about my life and business, using Oracle Cards to tap into what it was that I really wanted. This was a brand new experience for me. In my corporate life I was blindly following a path to promotion with the vague goal of being Marketing Director somewhere someday. Taking the time out of my busy schedule to think so intentionally about what I wanted felt like a luxury. Sitting there dreaming about the future, sharing it with a relative stranger and documenting it all in pictures on a vision board (I'd never heard of a vision board) was so much fun! And I felt that flutter of excitement again. I'll be honest, when she got the Oracle Cards out, I felt a sense of trepidation. I was worried they were tarot cards and that I was going to be involved in some kind of occult activity. I apologise now if you are a tarot reader - I had very limited knowledge of this kind of thing and my mum had always warned me away from anything that dabbled with spirits or fortune telling. I breathed a sigh of relief when my coach explained that Oracle Cards were simply to be used as prompts to help me tap into how I felt and thought about my past, present and future situation. We focussed on my business and the lifestyle I wanted. She asked me to close my eyes and took me through a beautiful meditation to help me connect with my intuition. When I opened my eyes and I looked at the cards that I had chosen, I was able to find meaning in the beautiful designs in relation to my life and business.

This all sounds very woo woo as I write this down but from this one session, I was powerfully moved! I kept coming back to visions of birds flying. I knew I wanted more time-freedom and holidays in the sun. It was a far cry from working in the dark mornings and evenings on projects I resented for relatively little financial compensation. I realised I'd built a business that wasn't serving me and I had to make big changes if I was to fly like the birds on my vision board.

I made a drastic decision. I let go of 90% of my clients that summer. The clients that I had stressed over detailed proposals for and my ex-employer who I'd gone through that sweaty negotiation to secure at a rate I was half happy with. I sacked my clients in the middle of a global pandemic with no other income secured to replace them. But the weirdest thing was, I didn't feel like this was a risk at all! I just knew that I didn't want to do that work any more and that I had to make space for something better. I was completely satisfied that releasing this work was the right decision. Just six months into running my own business full-time, I had my worst financial month so far. But I was free. I was mentally geared up, ready to fly, and there was no doubt in my mind that my wings wouldn't fail me. This was my intuition coming into play. I knew in my gut that saying "no" to work I didn't want to do, just because I had the skills to do it, was the right decision. But how was I going to replace all that lost income before I got in a financially sticky situation?

I didn't have any savings and I wasn't a power suit wearing entrepreneur that had gone out and secured financial backing to start up a business. It was just me, at my kitchen table on the second-hand laptop I'd bought from my old job for £50. Worse than that, I had debt because since returning to work part-time after maternity leave, I was strapped for cash all the time. I never asked anyone to give money to help start a business. I had to generate the funds to invest back into my business.

But thanks to tapping into my intuition I felt a sense of peace and purpose about letting this work go. I also knew what I wanted my revenue streams to look like and it was no longer 100% from 'done for you' client work.

As you're reading this, does my story resonate with you? From what I've seen with a lot of my clients and fellow *solopreneurs*, most small business owners go through the start-up phase making similar mistakes around choosing clients, pricing and managing their workload. It can be really challenging!

To help you take a quick temperature check of how satisfied you are with your business right now, grab a pen and paper and run through the following questions:

- In your business, what is enjoyable for you?
- What are you naturally good at? (Skills, abilities, gifts etcetera.) How do you use these skills in your business?
- What makes you feel successful?
- Are you chasing the money by doing work that you don't love (or actively dislike)?
- Who is important to you? How can your business support you to nurture your relationships?
- Looking at the future, how do you want to show up in your business, and what does alignment look like for you?

Chapter 2

Stepping into your zone of genius

After I let go of 90% of my clients and subsequently had my worst financial month to date in business, I rejoiced in finally having the time and creative space to focus on attracting the right people to work with. I chose a niche in my field - email marketing - and I said "no thank you" to the other digital marketing projects I was offered but didn't really want to do, and I made the commitment to put myself out there as an email marketer.

My decision to go all in on one marketing specialism and the subsequent action I took created two big results. Firstly, anyone who wanted help with email marketing came to me because this was my expertise and secondly, I got even better at email marketing which meant I could complete projects in less time and thus charge more money. Email marketing and copywriting became my zone of genius. As I got quicker at planning and writing email campaigns and I increased my prices; my hourly rate shot up to an amount I previously thought only lawyers were capable of charging.

My monthly income immediately took an upward swing and the big risk to let so many clients go was looking like it had paid off. I was very aware that I didn't want to build the same business I had just burned down and became very intentionally choosy about the kind of projects I would take on. It had to be the right project, for the right kind of client and at the right price point. As time went on, I received fewer enquiries from the types of businesses I didn't want to work with and I started to get ideal clients queuing up to work with me. It was like I'd put a big signal out to the Universe that I wasn't available for the work I had previously been struggling with and was only open to projects that befitted my new, choosy list of desirables. Of course, my marketing messaging was now signposting the ideal clients straight to me as well. Occasionally I'd be tested and an enquiry would come in that I didn't want to take on as a client. I wasn't fully out of my old scarcity mode so the money was always tempting and I had to tap into that intuition again and turn the work (and money) down.

Tapping into your intuition

I know it's easier said than done to spot the difficult, or the not-a-great-fit client then and turn down money. How can you start to trust your gut in business and use this inner "knowing" to help you decide if you want to work with someone or not? How do you know if it's a smart decision to say "no thank you" and if you're a people pleaser, how can you say "no" in a nice way?

Let's start with some guidance on how you can start to listen to your intuition. Sometimes it's as obvious as your brain highlighting all the red flags popping up in your initial conversations with a prospective client. Perhaps they're haggling on the money side already or they seem like they're going to have unreasonable expectations of you. Listen to the warning bells and act to stop the enquiry process before you get as far as quoting. This is where you politely decline or tell a white lie and say you're fully booked at the moment but will let them know when a spot opens up.

If the potential client seems nice but you just know you're not the best person to help them, it can make saying "no" a lot easier if you have someone else to refer them to. I used to do this all the time with e-commerce email marketing requests. I only worked with service-based businesses and I had a couple of people I would refer the product business leads on to. Both sides were grateful and I wasn't stuck trying to do a project that wasn't in my zone of genius.

Oftentimes, it's not immediately obvious whether a potential project or client is going to be a positive experience or one that will leave you wishing you'd turned it down. In situations where there's a niggle about whether you want to do the work or not, I recommend finding some head-space to let the decision work itself out in your mind. You can even try meditating on it. Stay with me! If you're not a fan of sitting in silence with nothing but your own thoughts for company, this practice will stretch you, but it's worth taking five minutes to help you make the best decision for you and your business in these scenarios.

Here's how you meditate on a business decision to let your intuition guide you to the best outcome:

1. Find five minutes alone time (away from anyone who might burst into the room and ask what's for dinner) and sit up straight in a chair with your feet on the ground.

2. Close your eyes and take a deep breath in through the nose, hold at the top and then out through the nose. Repeat this slow breathing and relax your mind; try to let any thoughts clear and just focus on the breath.
3. Next, imagine a root going down from your feet to the core of the earth - you are grounded.
4. Then visualise a bright light shooting out of the crown of your head up into the universe. You are now connected to your intuition!
5. Ask yourself the question: Do I want to work with this client? Stay with the question for a couple of minutes, remembering to breathe and staying connected to earth and sky.
6. Ask yourself: Can I help this client and get the result they need?
7. The answer will come through. It's usually the first response when you ask the question.

If you still struggle to gain clarity on what to do then try to put the money aside and think about the energy of the project. How will it feel for you to commit to working with this client?

You don't need to question every opportunity that comes along. Just the ones where you're feeling that something might be off or there are red flags and you want to be sure you're doing the best thing for you and your business if you take on the work.

I rarely need to question saying "yes" to a prospective client these days because every time I said "no thank you" has provided the time and energy to market my services to ideal clients more consistently. These days, all my marketing is geared up to attract the people I really want to work with. My messaging is very clear on who my services are for and why.

If you stay in the cycle of working with bad-fit clients just for the money, you won't have the resources left to make a change and start attracting well-paying dream clients instead. It has to stop somewhere.

Breaking up with clients

I'm well aware that you might not be as open to taking risks as I am! If the idea of letting go and turning down paying clients feels unachievable right now, then work on shifting your thoughts and energy around this by visualising what your business would look like if you only worked for perfect-fit clients who paid you well and paid you on time. It's really difficult to increase your prices for work you're already committed to doing for a client. When you're stuck undercharging, those clients aren't going to pay you much more (if anything) very willingly. To open the door for higher-paying clients, you have to let go of some of the dead wood. How can you do this? Well, one of the best 'get out of the bad-fit working relationship' clauses I've come up with was to deliver the break-up cliche of old: "It's not you, it's me". In business terms this simply looks like informing your clients that you're not going to be doing their kind of project work any more and send them to someone else who can help.

During my "Big Client Breakup of Summer 2020", I changed my services to only include email marketing. Then I let my clients know that I wouldn't be doing website copy/Social Media strategy/case study writing anymore. We wrapped up where we'd got to and it was goodbye. This process was made easier when I had someone else I could refer them to. Get your break-up script together and either hit SEND on that email or raise it on your next call. I bet that client will wish you well.

Where this gets tricky is when you like the type of work you're doing but you don't like the client. There's no easy excuse to terminate the working relationship before you've delivered your end of the deal. Of course, that client might be a nightmare because they're missing deadlines and it's become the never-ending project from hell. Most freelancers and service businesses have experienced this and there's only one way out. Hopefully you have a contract with milestone deadlines in it and you can let the client know that their time is up and give them a date when you will cease to work on their project because you have other work that's booked in.

You don't have to let go of 90% of your clients in one go like I did, but there are likely to be one or two clients killing your vibe and you're resenting doing the work. Start with them. Use the time that opens up when you're no longer at their beck and call or burning the midnight oil to complete their work; use it to craft a new offer and compelling messaging for your ideal client.

Still feeling resistance to making changes to your client base and offer? I get it! After all, you worked hard to win those clients and now I'm suggesting you might let them go - it feels uncomfortable and maybe even counter-intuitive to making your business a success.

To help you figure out what you really want your business to look like then take some time to journal on these questions:

- What would finding your stride in business look like for you?
- Where could you operate in your zone of genius?
- What type of businesses do you love to work with?
- Who is your favourite client right now and why?
- Which client takes the most from you and is starting to drain your resources and energy?

One of the biggest shifts to help you make more money in less time is turning down and letting go of the crap work so you have time to market yourself for the projects that feel easy-breezy to do. If you stay in the trap of taking on work you don't enjoy with clients who don't respect your time or boundaries, you're doing it for less compensation than you can realistically afford then scarcity will keep you in a chokehold. This could eventually cause your business to fail or even worse, you will be mentally or physically unable to carry on due to the stress it's creating.

Your Character Strengths

Once you've gained some clarity on who you would love to work with and the type of clients who aren't the best fit for you, it's time to turn your attention inwards once more and focus on what you're really good at and how you can harness your strengths at work.

Your first step on your strengths journey is to take the free VIA Character Strengths survey over at: www.viacharacter.org

Strengths psychology is about developing what we are naturally good at, instead of focusing on our weaknesses. When you build your business around your strengths, it feels more engaging and this engagement is key to creating a meaningful and happy life. More on this when we dive into Positive Psychology.

If your work is leaving you cold and you struggle to fully engage with it then taking the VIA survey will shed some light on where your strengths lie and enable you to come up with ideas on how you can bake the things you are really good at into your business. Take the survey and pin your top 10 strengths somewhere you can see them every day. It's worth paying for the full report to fully understand how your strengths might show up for you and what you can do to build on them.

If you're interested; my top 10 VIA Character Strengths are:

1. Humour
2. Gratitude
3. Hope
4. Forgiveness
5. Social Intelligence
6. Appreciation of Beauty & Excellence
7. Spirituality
8. Zest
9. Love
10. Fairness

Dream clients incoming; get ready to scale!

About six months after announcing my new niche of email marketing I now faced with a new problem that was really nice to have so early on in my business: I became fully booked. Even though I was committed to saying "no" to the wrong kind of clients for me, I was still maxed out with lovely people wanting their email strategy sorted and sequences written. It was time to look at creating a new revenue stream to help my clients get the results they wanted without me having to do all the work for them.

I'd previously run a 12-week online course teaching email marketing and this had been a great experience for me and I had happy clients from the programme. But running it as a live course meant anyone coming to me when it had already started, or after it had finished, didn't have any other way to access my knowledge and support. I decided to trial running a self-paced version of the programme so that I could enrol new clients as and when they came to me. In Chapter Six I share more about how I created this offer and crucially, how I found the time to plan, build and launch it while being fully booked.

This new programme became a key asset in my business to help me bring in more money without working more hours. It's well worth exploring how you could share your expertise with your clients so that they can do the work with your guidance, rather than you doing it all for them.

Finding the motivation to make changes

I've already shared with you that my original financial goal for my business was to match my pro-rated corporate salary which I did from the very first month I was fully self-employed. If I'd already hit this goal, why wasn't I content with staying fully booked? Why bother to create an online course and figure out new ways to make money? The answer is in part quite simple. It turns out that I'm very ambitious as a business owner and was so excited to see what was possible for normal people like me in this online business space, that I wanted a piece of that money-making action. This in itself had the potential to create a negative impact at home because I was so motivated to test new ways of making money, that I had started to squeeze work into any free pocket of time that I could find. In fact, it wasn't free time at all - I was sometimes choosing to work instead of being with my family. To prevent my business from taking over my life, I needed to come back to my Big Why.

To arrive at WHY I'm currently doing what I'm doing, I need to give you a little more background on what happened before I left my day job to go freelance. Before I was approached about doing some marketing work on the side I'd already been experimenting with some extracurricular ways to make money. I'd been flipping clothes on eBay and Depop for a few months in an effort to top up my part-time salary in my spare time. If you don't know what flipping is, it's where you buy an item for cheap and resell it for a profit. I'd made a few hundred quid until I realised that with all the time I spent scouring charity shops, washing, ironing, taking photos and creating the listings, I wasn't making a very good hourly rate at all. I once found a Burberry jumper in a local charity shop for £4 that I sold for £45 and that was probably the height of my flipping career. So, when my ex-colleague got in touch about supporting her marketing project, I was already open to ideas for making some extra cash. It turned out that doing marketing (the thing I had twelve years experience in already) was far more lucrative than reselling clothes. I re-donated to the charity shop a bunch of stuff I couldn't sell and decided the life of a professional flipper wasn't for me. I was curious about alternative ways to make money but I had no desire to leave my job and become responsible for my own income. Why then, had I left my job just nine months later to run my own business?

The catalyst for leaving my safe job wasn't actually the lure of making more money. It was a chance conversation at the office water cooler that changed the course of my career for good. A work friend and I were chatting about our kids and she casually mentioned that before I knew it, I'd be choosing a school for Penny. I hadn't given schools much thought at this point as Penny was only two and it felt like school was a long time away. Then my friend dropped the bomb that gave me such a strong reaction, I felt it right in the pit of my stomach. She said: "And of course you'll need to look at which schools do out-of-school clubs." Right then in that moment, my inner voice replied "NOPE". I wasn't going to do it. I wasn't going to put Penny in breakfast and after-school clubs or use a childminder. I was going to be the one doing the school run and we were going to hang out every day after school together before she became a teenager and probably disowned me. I also realised then (had I been living under a rock?) that my annual leave wouldn't cover school holidays. I didn't quite know what the answer was but as I nodded and smiled at my work friend I knew that somehow I wasn't going to be working 9-5, rushing around trying to juggle school hours and my career. I had a deep sense of knowing that something else would happen. I honestly didn't know what - but I knew I wouldn't be needing childcare around school.

I feel like the Universe was on my side after this light-bulb-water-cooler moment. I was open to a new way of living my life that meant I could fit work around my priorities as a parent. I never contemplated NOT working, I just knew something else would come along. I think the Universe responded to the energy I was putting out there by sending some side work my way - just to see how I got on with it! The rest is history and on that first day of school when Adam and I walked Penny to her class, I felt like I'd made it in life. I was living my dream of being available to walk my daughter to and from school every day and she would be at home with me during the holidays. My goal wasn't to make lots of money, it was just about being at home with Penny.

I know that for a lot of parents, working super short days so they can be at home isn't their dream at all! And that's OK. The reason I share my story is because whether or not you want to work ten hours a week or you're cool with sixty hours, as soon as it starts to become all about the money, the wheels can start to fall off in business. Money will only motivate you so far. It's time to get clear on your Big Why.

Why do you want to run your own business?

I first started learning about Positive Psychology in early 2022 and it radically changed my approach to work; in terms of how I prioritise my well-being and the things that are important to me over striving for success in my business. At the same time as getting clear on what I wanted my life to look like, I made more progress because Positive Psychology helped me to tap into the motivation to work towards my goals. If you ever feel like you're just going through the motions, getting some Positive Psychology coaching will help you to understand what's really important to you and how to feel more fulfilled and happy. This doesn't necessarily mean setting less ambitious financial goals but I do think that for many, we can get caught up chasing the money and lose sight of other things that contribute to us leading a meaningful and happy life.

At this point in my entrepreneurial career, as I started to redefine what success looks like for me and map out a more enjoyable journey towards my ambitious goals, I became fired up to share this work with more business owners - hence writing this book!

But first, let's rewind to the summer of 2022 because this is when I decided to train as a certified Positive Psychology Coach. I signed up to a certification programme because I was witnessing many of my clients struggling with their mindset and it was affecting how successfully they were able to implement the marketing strategies I was giving them. I knew I had to do something to help my clients show up with confidence and find motivation to keep going when they were faced with challenges or failures. I wanted to be equipped to take my clients through a proper coaching process, instead of just sharing what was working for me.

If there was ever an example I could give you of being 'Positively Productive', the summer of 2022 saw me embody this. I undertook over 125 hours of learning, practice coaching and assessments to certify as a coach. I did eight weeks of practice coaching in the evenings after Penny was in bed as my coaching buddy was also a business owner and she had two young girls of her own. Our kids were off school because it was school holidays and this was also during an intense heatwave where temperatures soared to 40 degrees here in the UK. My buddy was based in Ibiza and she was just as hot and tired as I was! Throughout the study, showing up for online classes and handing in the assessment at the end of the course, I kept my eye on the goal of getting certified and what this would mean for my business. I had strong motivation to do the work and be ready to blend this new skill with my marketing expertise because I knew that I wanted to learn more about harnessing the Power of Positivity. My clients needed it and it would be a good way to differentiate myself from other marketers.

To meet all the milestones to get certified alongside running my business and parenting during the summer holidays I implemented the time management strategies I'm sharing with you in this book. For example, before school was out for summer I blocked out Monday afternoons for Positive Psychology study as I knew I was extra productive on Mondays. I scheduled early morning study blocks to work through each module before my family woke up and the daily hustle of getting out the door for school began. This time to study was in my calendar so I didn't often feel overwhelmed by the sheer volume of the undertaking because I could see that it had a place in my schedule. If my workload started to feel like it was running away from me, at the end of every day I'd shuffle my calendar around, eliminate tasks, delegate tasks and make it work. The assessments were all due in August and my daughter was at home with me the entire time. We even took a week's holiday at Center Parcs and I dialled into that week's training session from the forest! As I write this down, I can't quite believe I did all that study and passed the certification with such limited "alone time" available. But with careful planning and strong motivation I did it - you can harness this energy too when you tap into the thing that truly motivates you.

In this book I'm sharing practical advice on how you can take on big projects, learn new skills, or do anything you've previously dismissed because you thought you didn't have time. You don't need to sacrifice your own well-being or quality time with your loved ones either. You have the resources available to you and my hope is the following Chapters will help you to achieve anything that you have a desire for.

Working out your Why

I've already shared my belief that focusing on the money will only get you so far in business. But if it isn't the money goal that will bring you success, then what is it? First you need to understand what success really means to you and extend this beyond making money. This is not as simple as it sounds! Since deciding I wanted to run my own business to be at home with Penny, I then got super excited by the prospect of making an incredible amount of money and I've been around in circles battling with what success really looks like for me. Then I discovered the Positive Psychology approach to well-being and living a happy life.

Let me introduce you to Professor Martin Seligman. Prof Seligman is a leading researcher in the field of Positive Psychology and his research covers three forms of happy lives: a pleasant life, a life of engagement and a life of meaning. I won't go into all three areas in this book because Seligman has written over thirty books on this topic and you can find out more from the source if you're keen to broaden your knowledge. For the purposes of helping you gain some clarity on WHY you're running your business, let's look at Meaning.

Studies have shown that to have a sense of meaning then we need to feel that what we do is valuable and worthwhile. Just reading that sentence might bring up plenty of questions for you about the work you do in your business. Taking it one step further; to have meaning also requires the sense of belonging to and/or serving something that we believe is greater than ourselves. This might be possible through your business with the resources that it affords you in your personal life to give time, expertise or money to a project or community close to your heart.

Getting clear on your meaning and purpose in life can take time and for most people (myself included), it's not easy. I struggled for weeks to define my meaning and purpose during my Positive Psychology certification because I had the misconception that it should be world-changing. Through hours of coaching and self-reflection I kept returning to my desire to be a present parent for my daughter and to experience as much quality time with my family as possible. When this first came up for me, I dismissed it as too small for my meaning in life. Surely I should be using my entrepreneurial powers for the good of the wider world instead of wanting to take my family on holiday? I carried on learning and broadened my understanding of meaning and purpose.

As I learned more about the pillars of a meaningful life, my studies introduced me to the idea that experiencing belonging is a key component of life satisfaction and happiness. I dug into this and I found a strong sense of belonging in my identity as a mum. Again, I initially tried to dismiss this because in the cut and thrust world of business kids slow you down and I thought mum life surely didn't qualify as the space I should belong to the most. I couldn't see how this would bring success in my business. Was my purpose supposed to focus on being a mum or being a business owner? Could I be both and be "successful"? I kept circling back to what success means for me.

As I read more about belonging and understood how my role as a parent fits in with my meaning and purpose I finally accepted that for me to live my best, most fulfilled life, my version of success needed to include my family as much as possible. I was going against this by focusing on the money and resenting that I wasn't making as much money as I might whilst I was busy being a mum.

As I peeled back the layers, I also realised that I stood for generosity and I want to help others and share my good fortune. In my business, my mission was to help others to live their best lives at home and in their business through supporting them with their marketing strategy and the Positive Psychology coaching I could offer alongside it. I want to help people have their fair share of the good things in this world. And I want to do this working only twenty hours a week and not putting Penny into childcare outside of school. As soon as I got clear on this mission, I felt excited! I wrote down in my journal that building my business on my own terms and having it provide us with the fun experiences together as a family made me feel successful. I felt motivated at the prospect of using my business to give us this quality of life and to be able to say "I did it" without making sacrifices that would ultimately be too big a cost for me.

I also realised that my spirit of wanting to help others could look like giving my time and charitable donations to my local community and to Penny's school. I'm motivated to make my corner of the world a little better and this excited me a lot more than trying to set a huge goal to become an international philanthropist.

I don't expect you to find the answer to your life's meaning and purpose right here right now but I'm here to point you in the right direction by exploring this for yourself, and, I hope by sharing my experience of trying to define this brings it to life a little bit as I think meaning can often feel like a lofty concept.

The following journaling prompts may help you to work out your Big Why:

- What makes you feel most alive?
- What do you stand for?
- What can you do better than 90% of people?

- What value do you create?
- What is your zone of genius?
- What problem do you hate to see in the world?
- What motivates you?
- What relationships in your life are important to you?

Looking over your responses to these questions will help you to understand what is most important. Not what you think *should* be most important (like making money!). From this you can start to define your meaning and purposeful goals in life and business and get clear on your Big Why.

Chapter 3
Beating procrastination

As we've been exploring WHY you're running your own business and what success looks like to you, let's change gears and explore the practical side of running your business; including content marketing, and how you're going to find the time to implement everything that's going to keep you on the path to success. But first, a word of caution on one of the biggest drains of your time and creative energy in business...

The big distraction

Whether or not you think you're pretty good at setting boundaries with how much time you spend on your phone, tablet or laptop, I bet there are improvements you can make here to become both more productive and more creative. The time you spend glued to a screen has a direct impact on how much time you have to get stuff done or how energised you feel to do it. Helping you to make tweaks to how and when you access your various devices with a view to opening up more time to dedicate to your business is the purpose of this Chapter.

I'm going to hold my hands up right now and let you know that I'm a smug iPhone user. Don't hate me; but I feel smug because I never look at my phone in bed at night because I know it affects sleep quality and I don't pick it up first thing in the morning. I don't check my socials to see what disaster has befallen the world overnight or my inbox to see four hundred plus emails waiting for a reply. I wait until I've had my protein porridge before I tackle or ignore those things. I feel like everyone around me is glued to their phones while I'm enjoying the scenery or architecture or just people watching. I'll confess, I judge people who are scrolling when in my opinion, they should be comfortable in the present moment with only their mind for company. Don't even get me started on people who watch stuff on their phones when they're out for dinner with their partner or friends. But this is modern life and not judging people is a work in progress for me.

For the purposes of being Positively Productive, I want to help you shine a light on your phone usage in the context of you as an entrepreneur because it has an impact on both how productive you can be AND how positive you feel. How positive you feel when you sit down to work has a direct effect on your productivity. And yes, this self-examination will include assessing hard facts about your Social Media usage. I suspect that if you have a Social Media presence then chances are you spend more time attending to it than you're comfortable with.

Despite finding my current screen time sweet spot thanks to the boundaries I keep with my phone, at the end of my first year in business I had a wake up call with screen time. I'd never checked the screen time report on my iPhone before, and after a particularly busy week, which ended with an epic 'to do' list giving me stress, I was prompted to check my screen time. I was curious to see where my time was going and I was shocked at what I discovered! According to the stats, I had been spending an average of twenty-four hours a week on my phone. I have twenty hours for my work so I had to ask myself the serious question: was screen time eating into my working day? Was I actually working forty-four hours a week instead of my perceived twenty? Was spending twenty-four hours holding my phone the reason I'd not read as many books as I'd like to so far that year? Honestly, this floored me. The most confounding part was that I would swear to you I was only spending maybe two hours a day on my phone. Which would be fourteen hours a week. That still feels like a lot but it is what it is, right? I stream music from my phone, my shopping list is on there, and of course, check work emails on the go.

Realising that I'd grossly underestimated how long I was using my phone made me suspect I was unconsciously wasting a lot of time. I dug further and had to do a double take. The stats showed for that particularly busy week, I had been on my phone for over twenty-nine hours! Over a full day and night on my phone. Madness! I actually felt ashamed. I'm a grown-up, a parent and a business owner - what excuse did I have for staring at my phone for twenty-nine hours in one week?

I use my laptop for most work tasks so I knew that phone screen time didn't include speaking to clients and it definitely didn't include writing marketing copy or strategising about revenue streams for the year ahead. I had all kinds of projects on the back burner and I immediately resolved to change my phone habits and get some head-space to move the projects that will help me scale my business to the 'done' pile.

At this point in the story of my personal screen time shame, I imagine you've either grabbed your phone to check your report or you're about to check once you've finished reading this Chapter.

I emailed my subscribers about this at the time and I got so many replies sharing their stats and reflections with me. I invite you to do the same (if you like!). Drop me an email kelly@cheerupmarketing.com and share your average weekly screen time. High or low - go for it.

Seeing the cold hard facts about how many hours I was staring at my phone was the wake-up call I needed to change my behaviour. I'd already been making tweaks to my time management as I got to grips with running a business or how I organised my working week around my three-year-old, but I still felt like I was playing catch up with work tasks. Now I could see where a lot of my time was going, I felt relieved and excited that I had an opportunity to claw back hours of time every week. This is one of the reasons why I'm sharing this story with you - you're potentially on the brink of making quick changes right this very week to free up hours of your time! This is an exciting opportunity.

I went a level deeper with my iPhone stats and the report showed me that out of the twenty-nine hours I'd spent on my phone that week; eight hours and thirty-four minutes of that time was on Instagram, with five hours forty on Facebook. To me this was unacceptable! Yes, I was using Social Media for work but fourteen hours across two Social Media platforms in one week? I couldn't say this was all work which was ultimately going to contribute to the money I was making in my business. I knew then that I was mindlessly scrolling for way longer than I had had estimated.

When you take a look at your own screen time report make a note of the top three apps where you're spending most of your time. Ask yourself: are you happy with dedicating that much time to those apps? If, like me, you don't want to give quite so much of your precious time to your phone, keep reading because I have some hacks to help you cut down screen time. We're also going to get into smart content marketing strategies that will mean you can still raise your profile online whilst cutting your Social Media usage.

We are powerless to resist these apps, or are we?

I spent a long time believing that I was manipulated to the point of being unable to resist the draw of Instagram and Facebook because the genius app developers knew how to keep me coming back to check these apps. I haven't seen the 2020 documentary *The Social Dilemma* (partly because I didn't want to feel "seen"), but I get the gist. Of course there are some very clever people working on how to get you to spend more time on their app, but I've come to think about apps and screen time in a different way which has helped me to take some of my power back.

I'll share my thought process around phone usage during your precious work time as it might help you too. Here's a new way to consider what picking up your phone and checking your notifications and opening apps during work time means: **you are making the choice to be distracted.** Challenge your belief that you are being controlled by the genius app developers or Mark Zuckerberg. You do have a choice. You are choosing to check your phone instead of concentrating on the task at hand. Sit with that realisation for a while. By becoming aware of your choice to be distracted you can begin to stop yourself in your tracks and refuse to be pulled away from what you know you should be doing.

Here's what the science says about getting back on track after checking one tiny notification on your phone. A study by the University of California, Irvine found that it takes an average of twenty-three minutes and fifteen seconds to get yourself back on track after being interrupted.

This means that even if you only give in to the temptation to react to a notification or tap the Facebook app just a few times a day, you lose an hour of work. We don't have time for that.

OK, I can tell you're now feeling fired up to NEVER be distracted by your devices ever again. Like you, I can't believe I was ever such a chump to give in so easily when I know I have important work to get done. With all this in mind, and as intelligent entrepreneurs, why do we choose to be distracted? This can be down to a number of reasons and I've started to see a pattern when I reach for my phone for a quick scroll. Usually it's because:

- The phone notifies me that something is waiting for me to look at. *Have I made a sale?*

Has someone commented on my post? Does a client need my help?

- I'm about to undertake a boring task and I'm putting it off (think tackling my accounting spreadsheet)
- I'm about to do a mentally challenging task and I'm putting it off (like writing a ten-email sales sequence - phew! That's a lot of writing I've got to do)

Being distracted by notifications has a simple solution if you choose to address it for the good of your concentration and productivity - turn them off. My pings were even more distracting because they came through to my Apple watch, making my wrist vibrate and light up every time someone commented or liked my post. This had to stop.

Secondly, you can delete apps if you find them too tempting. I had to take Facebook off my phone and only use it on desktop because I was like a moth to a flame when it came to tapping it on my phone. I found that after a few months, I was able to put the app back on my phone and I'd broken the habit of tapping the app multiple times a day.

If you find yourself reaching for some light Social Media relief (or Candy Crush!) ahead of boring or challenging tasks, try implementing a new set of rules:

1. Recognise that by picking up the phone, you are CHOOSING not to get the task done. You are allowing yourself to be distracted. Are you OK with that? Are you a person who is easily distracted or a person who gets things done? What kind of entrepreneur do you need to be to succeed? A distracted or focussed person?
2. Ahead of starting the task, put your phone in another room. Next level tip: I lock mine in the boot of my car - it's extra effort to leave the house and unlock the car to retrieve it.
3. Use Positive Psychology to boost your energy ahead of the draining task. Check out the Red Activities and Green Activities intervention at the end of this Chapter.
4. Set yourself a goal of how long you are going to spend on the task and time track (using Toggl) as you go.
5. For tasks where you really want to get it over and done with then consider using the Pomodoro technique until it's complete. Check out my Positively Productive spin on

this time management exercise at the end of this Chapter.

I'll reiterate; you are choosing to be distracted by your phone from a task that will move your business forward and make you more money. Once I started to look at my phone in this way I took my power back! I'm not content to languish in a Social Media bubble as time ticks away and I'm no closer to my goal. Are you? Of course not! Whether or not this is simply getting client work done (to get paid) or creating a new revenue stream for the business, Social Media scrolling and playing games will get in the way of you getting this done.

Exercise: Red Activities and Green Activities

I'm excited to share how you can use Positive Psychology to boost your energy ahead of tasks that you find challenging or draining. Your first step is to identify which tasks give you energy and which tasks leave you feeling depleted. The effect that certain tasks have on you is tied into your personal strengths and weaknesses - if you haven't yet taken free VIA Character Strengths survey to find out what your strengths are, you can do so over at: www.viacharacter.org

I recommend paying for the full report as you'll find it brings to life how your strengths come into play in life and at work. The free report will still give you some great insights.

Strengths Psychology is fascinating and it sits under the Engagement Pillar of Positive Psychology. The exercise I invite you to try out here will shine a light on why some tasks in your business seem to take forever or never make it off your 'to do' list. These tasks could be important steps on the path to your goals so we need to tackle how you approach areas of your work that feel difficult, or where you can't seem to gain traction.

When we increase our engagement in life and work research has shown this gives us greater positive feelings and satisfaction. This matters in matters of how productive we can be; the research also found a strong link between engagement and motivation. If you aren't engaged with the tasks at hand then you probably don't feel motivated to start or complete it. Ready to show up in your business with more motivation? It's time to identify which tasks fill your cup and which ones drain it quicker than me drinking an iced latte on a hot day.

Exercise: Red and Green Activities

The goal of this exercise is to increase your awareness of activities that rely on your strengths or weaknesses. Take the VIA Character Strengths survey at www.viacharacter.org to download your personal strengths report. You can also look at Gallup's CliftonStrengths:

https://www.gallup.com/cliftonstrengths

Activities that rely on our strengths are enjoyable so when we're working on the task at hand we feel as if our energy levels are being boosted.

The opposite applies to activities that require skills that are our weaknesses. These activities often feel draining and leave us depleted of energy.

Instructions

Step 1 - Gaining Awareness of your Red and Green Activities

A key sign of when your strengths come into play is the energy you feel. When we use our strengths we feel energised and engaged. Activities that rely on our strengths are enjoyable and feel as if our energy levels are being raised. The opposite applies when we are using our weaknesses; it drains the energy out of us. When we operate from our weaknesses we often feel negativity, disengagement, and lack of motivation.

In this exercise we call activities that rely on your strengths and provide you energy "green activities."

These are activities that:

- You genuinely enjoy doing
- Make you feel energised
- Make you forget the time
- You look forward to
- You can do well even under conditions of stress or fatigue

Activities that rely on your weaknesses and deplete your energy are referred to as "red activities."

These are activities that:

- You do not like doing

- Make you feel depleted
- Seem to pass very slowly
- You don't look forward to
- Require a lot of effort and self-control to do well

Step 2: Record Red and Green Moments

Over the next 7 days record your "green" and "red" moments, by providing a brief description of the activity and the energy levels you felt whilst engaged in the activity. You can indicate your energy level by putting one of the signs below:

-- Required a lot of energy
- Required some energy
Ø Did not require energy but did not give energy either
+ Gave me positive energy
++ Gave me a lot of positive energy

DAY 1

GREEN ACTIVITIES		
Activity	Energy Levels	Notes

RED ACTIVITIES		
Activity	Energy Levels	Notes

DAY 2

GREEN ACTIVITIES		
Activity	Energy Levels	Notes

RED ACTIVITIES		
Activity	Energy Levels	Notes

DAY 3

GREEN ACTIVITIES		
Activity	Energy Levels	Notes

RED ACTIVITIES		
Activity	Energy Levels	Notes

DAY 4

GREEN ACTIVITIES		
Activity	Energy Levels	Notes

RED ACTIVITIES		
Activity	Energy Levels	Notes

DAY 5

GREEN ACTIVITIES		
Activity	Energy Levels	Notes

RED ACTIVITIES		
Activity	Energy Levels	Notes

DAY 6

GREEN ACTIVITIES		
Activity	Energy Levels	Notes

RED ACTIVITIES		
Activity	Energy Levels	Notes

DAY 7

GREEN ACTIVITIES		
Activity	Energy Levels	Notes

RED ACTIVITIES		
Activity	Energy Levels	Notes

Step 3: Strengths and Weakness Reflection

After completing the reflections examine closely your answers. **Select the five activities that make you feel most energised** and the most depleted from, add them to the table:

MY TOP 5 GREEN ACTIVITIES	
Activities that make me feel most energised	Strength (s) Used

MY TOP 5 RED ACTIVITIES	
Activities that make me feel most depleted	Strength (s) Unused

Step 4: Evaluation

What have you learned from this exercise?

How can you use your strengths more often?

How can you effectively deal with situations that deplete your energy? For instance, can you delegate your energy-draining areas to someone or reframe those tasks? Alternatively you may marshal your strengths to help or build energy ahead of time so that you have the baseline you need to get through an energy-draining task.

Once you've completed seven days of tracking your red and green activities you will start to understand why you are easily distracted when you attempt certain tasks, or why you feel like a vampire has been at you after completing certain types of work.

In an ideal world you would delegate and outsource all your red tasks to someone else, but the reality is we perhaps don't have the budget for this right away or actually, some tasks can only be done by you. Therefore we could benefit from having a tool to help bolster our energy ahead of red tasks and restore us afterwards. Hopefully you came up with some ideas of ways you can use your specific strengths to build your energy around your energy-draining tasks. If you are struggling to come up with ideas then here are some of the ways I give myself an energy boost ahead of tackling jobs that I find tiring or just plain boring.

My Positively Productive energy boosters

1. My top VIA Character Strength is Humour. Usually this comes into play when I'm around other people as I can't resist trying to make people laugh. Therefore a great way for me to replenish my energy after a red task is to hang out with people who tickle my funny bone, so to speak. Luckily I married a guy who I find hilarious so I tend to get a humour top-up most days if he's on form. Other activities I'll diarise around my energy-draining days in the office include nights out with my best mate or sisters. Having a fun social engagement to look forward to in my diary gives me the motivation to get the job done so that I can fully enjoy it.
2. Gratitude is number two on my strengths profile. I practise gratitude every single day by writing down three things I'm grateful for just before I go to sleep at night. The timing of this means I don't use it immediately before a red activity but I credit a consistent gratitude practice with boosting my overall feelings of engagement with the life I've

created and I wake up most days feeling motivated and ready to rock and roll.

3. I'm a member of a very nice gym which boasts a sauna, steam room and cafe with baristas that make a perfect cappuccino. I've discovered that by attending the 9.30 a.m. Strength and Conditioning class, I can achieve amazing progress on red activities for the following hour. I take a shower and then get set up in the cafe with my coffee. Full of post-exercise endorphins, even the most challenging or repetitive tasks feel like a breeze. In fact, I ride high on that boost of well-being all day. Nothing can bring me down! I've worked out that by 'losing' an hour and fifteen minutes of the working day to attend the 9.30 a.m. class, I more than make up for it afterwards in productivity. During busy weeks, I used to feel guilty about taking time off work to go to the gym. After all, I only have until 2.30 p.m. before it's school run time again! I've tested how my day pans out by missing the class to power through in the office and I always regret it, ending the day feeling depleted. I've committed space in my calendar for two 9.30 a.m. classes a week and my productivity has never been better.

A few mini energy boosts I implement daily when at work:

- A three-to-five-minute meditation using the Insight Timer app
- Dancing around the room to one of my favourite songs
- Making a nice coffee - I grind the beans and use an Aeropress
- Four rounds of Box Breathing (in for four, hold for four, out for four, hold for four)
- A power walk around the block
- Read a few pages of a book I find inspiring (I love *Notes From The Universe* or *The Game Of Life And How To Play It* for a quick pick-me-up)

Hopefully these examples give you some creative inspiration to find your own energy boosters to tackle those red tasks with limited fatigue.

How to Pomodoro - Positively Productive style!

The Pomodoro Technique is a staple of the time management world and although I don't advocate 'powering through' as a sustainable way to get all your work done; the Pomodoro technique definitely has its time and place and I do implement it occasionally in my business. Usually when tackling a large copywriting project like a sales page or email sequence!

If you're familiar with the technique, keep reading because I have a Positively Productive spin I encourage you to try next time you use it. If you don't know how to Pomodoro, this is how it works (with my tried and tested hacks included in italics):

1. Choose a task you need to work on
2. *Positively Productive hack: Lock your phone in your car! Or put it well out of reach and hearing.*
3. Set a timer for twenty-five minutes and begin work. Do not veer away from the task at hand - keep a singular focus on the one thing you want to get done
4. When the twenty-five minutes are up, set a timer for five minutes and take a break. *Positively Productive Hack: Do NOT pick up your phone or check your email during these five minutes! Stay away from reading anything that will derail your train of thought for the upcoming twenty-five minutes of work. Instead, make a drink, fold laundry, dance around the room, go outside and get some fresh air*
5. Begin the next twenty-five minute period of focussed work
6. Take another five-minute break
7. Begin your third and final round of twenty-five minutes' focussed work
8. You are done! *Positively Productive hack: The traditional Pomodoro technique states you take a longer break of fifteen to thirty minutes here then go back to twenty-five*

minutes on, five off for a further three rounds. I've never managed to Pomodoro for more than three rounds so don't feel that you have to push yourself to do it if you are feeling depleted at this point. You've just completed seventy-five minutes focussed work - well done!

Chapter 4

The Social Media marketing trap

Now that I've given Social Media a bashing for being too distracting, I feel it's only fair to give credit where it's due: as a small business owner, Social Media is a fantastic way to connect with potential customers. It makes digital marketing accessible to entrepreneurs from non-marketing backgrounds who can immediately start to share what they sell, without needing a website.

When I launched Cheer Up Marketing, I built my own website using Squarespace after mapping out the page content and then copywriting the entire thing myself. I knew how to do this thanks to having twelve years' involvement with website design, user journey and copywriting for the web for every business I'd ever worked for. I have a basic knowledge of HTML and in the day job I'd absorbed a decent amount of information about what makes a good website thanks to collaborating with web design experts over the years. When it was time for me to knock up a decent-looking, easy-to-navigate website for my own business, I found it relatively easy and also fun because I was in control of the branding (I made it pastel-coloured).

But my brand new website wasn't ranking on Google from day one and I knew I would need multiple marketing channels to reach my ideal clients. To help me get some reach straight away I created an Instagram account and Facebook company page. I decided I was brave enough to risk boring my Facebook friends and family with business-related content and converted my personal profile from photos of me on wild nights out to become a shop window for my personal brand - I'm a marketer for hire!

As solo entrepreneurs starting businesses from our kitchen tables with zero budget we are so lucky to have Social Media marketing tools available to us.

The online world is our digital marketing oyster. But there's a very risky marketing strategy I see small businesses using day in, day out: putting 90% of sales hopes and dreams on Social Media. If you don't have a thorough understanding of where your ideal client is or how they consume digital media then you can easily waste years of your life pumping all your creativity and time into Social Media marketing which fails to bring home the bacon. I see businesses fail every week where they announce (on Social Media) they are having to close down because they simply aren't making enough. And this makes me feel SO frustrated because chances are, that person is great at what they do but they're failing to reach the right people or communicate the benefits of their offer in a way that makes it a no-brainer purchase decision.

Say you do manage to break through the noise and the dreaded Social Media algorithm and start to see engagement with your content and at last - some quality leads come in. Maybe you break the five thousand followers mark (at the time of writing this I'm only just over three thousand on Instagram) or the heady heights of ten thousand followers. You've made it! Or have you? What happens when Meta rolls out the next big algorithm change and your reach plummets? This year we have the blue tick available to purchase - I now pay £11.99 a month to have a verified Instagram account because I'm testing what this does for my reach. Threads was launched as I was finishing editing this book. Social Media marketing is a fickle beast and you have zero control over who sees your content and when. On top of this, you do not own your Social Media followers and they can be taken away from you at any moment. We all know someone who got hacked and lost all their followers. If they were making money from Social Media, that revenue stream is gone overnight. This is not smart marketing - this is building your business on ground that you do not own.

What should you do instead? Throw your phone out the window and commit to a full-on digital detox? Start sending flyers out in the post? Not at all. If you're reading this and you've realised you've put way too many marketing eggs in the Social Media basket, don't panic. I'm about to give you a new direction which will alleviate that risk.

Firstly, if you don't have a website yet - get on it and create one. I know, I know, you're not a techy person and building your own website sounds like a lot of hard work. It doesn't have to be. Start by choosing your domain name - mine is cheerupmarketing.com and I also own the .co.uk - and snap it up before someone else does. There are dozens of DIY website tools and templates you can use to create your online home and start to get found on Google. I'm not particularly techy either but I'm happy to share what I did. I signed up to Squarespace, selected a template I liked the look of and would work for content focussed on services because I have no physical product to showcase. I selected the template and simply swapped out the placeholder images and text for my own.

Pro tip: you are going to need professional photos of yourself for your website unless you want it to look like you built it yourself with no web design experience. Nothing elevates an out-the-box website template than proper photos of you. Don't use selfies or corporate head-shots from that work photo-shoot you had five years ago - it will look unprofessional and you won't feel excited about sharing it with the world.

Pay close attention to this next part because I can pretty much guarantee that if you've been using Social Media as your main marketing channel, you won't have been doing this. I want you to start creating long-form content for your own channels first. We are no longer giving Zuckerberg first dibs on your best, most creative content. Instead, you're going to focus your time on creating content for the marketing channels you DO have control over. By this I mean your blog (yes, I know you don't have a blog yet -

you're about to start one) and your email list (same as the blog - you're going to get this going right away). Not a fan of the written word? That's cool - you can create video or audio content and then get it transcribed and tidied up for your blog. This becomes the content you'll share with your email subscribers.

Invest your time in creating content that sticks around for longer than a few days. Consider adding a podcast or YouTube channel into the mix. Not sure which one is best for you? Start by asking your ideal clients how they consume content and which creators they follow. Podcast and YouTube content is searchable for years after you've hit publish! It beats a carefully curated Instagram feed hands down in terms of longevity.

Once you've flipped your content creative process on its head and you're producing long-form content first, Social Media can then have the by-product of this new stream of creativity. You can chop up your blogs, podcasts and videos into neat sound-bites and written posts and dine out on those for weeks. Gone are the days of chalking up hours of time creating engaging Social Media posts only to witness them disappear into the abyss of the never-ending scroll. Take back your creative power and pour it into long-form content because over time, this will bring organic traffic to your website and help you grow an email list of ideal clients. Doing content marketing this way around ensures you are building solid foundations for your business rather than relying on a platform you don't own or control to do all the lead generation leg work for you.

Let's focus on email marketing for a minute. It's totally different to Social Media marketing. For starters, you own the data you collect about your subscribers. They are opting in to hear from you and when you store their name and email address in a reputable email marketing provider (like Mailerlite, Mailchimp or Convertkit etcetera) you can export that data if you ever need to. An email list is a tangible business asset that adds monetary value to your company if you were ever to sell up. You don't get paid for Social Media subscribers because your business doesn't own that data. On Social Media, your business is the product because your information is being sold to other businesses to allow them to market to you using paid ads.

From this point onwards I don't want your marketing 'to do' list to read: Create Instagram posts for June. At the top of your list, I want you to plan one stellar piece of content that talks to one key thing your ideal client must understand about you and the value of the work that you do to make them want to become a customer. Radical, I know.

This is one of my favourite hacks for staying consistently visible online in less time than it takes to write a month's worth of Social Media captions. My monthly content plan is a one-page Google doc in which I document my overarching topic for the month, the blogs I'll write about that topic, the emails I'll send about that topic and the offers that I'm selling that month. It all links together and has a sales strategy behind it. Ask yourself the question: for the thing that I'm asking my audience to buy from me over the coming weeks and months, what must they understand about it to move them along the journey to making that purchase? Write about that thing and put it across every channel where your ideal client is hanging around.

Pro tip: not sure where your clients are hanging out online? Run a focus group where you ask them what Social Media platforms they are most active on, what blogs they read, podcasts they listen to, people they like to follow or where they network. Then show up as best you can in those places. The confidence that comes with making the decision to not bother with LinkedIn any more because you know your ideal clients are on Instagram and prefer to read blogs will have you fired up to create content and show up in those places.

You have my permission to show up on Social Media when you know that's where you're going to reach your customers but with this comes the risk of losing time to the scroll. Remember that the researchers have found you don't just lose scrolling time, you lose twenty extra minutes getting back to where you left off. I've already shared some hacks with you to avoid the scroll hole, and when you get the budget, here's how you can take your boundaries around Social Media to a much more professional level: outsource community management and posting content. I did this just eight months into running my business. I hired a virtual assistant (VA) and tasked her with managing my Facebook group, creating all the visuals for social posts and getting the content scheduled.

Nothing makes me feel more like a boss than when I'm out and about enjoying quality time with my loved ones or precious alone time in the sauna than to know that whilst I'm living my life, my Social Media profiles are being populated with content on auto-pilot and it wasn't even me who had to organise that schedule. Paying my virtual assistant to do this for me is the reason my content goes out on time. Crucially, she does all the image creation so I don't have to go anywhere near Canva - another tool famous for being a creative time drain. If you're partial to faffing in Canva, I invite you to time track every minute you spend there and then add up both your hourly rate for doing so and the impact on the time taken away from revenue-generating tasks in your business. Ready to drop Canva like a hot cake? Great! Get a VA who knows their way around a brand palette and what looks good on the *'gram* and let them take that job off your 'to do' list. Feels good, doesn't it?

I currently have two Facebook groups - one for clients and one to bring in leads specifically for my email marketing programme. I know I'm a sucker for scrolling Facebook so I have my VA go into both groups and if there's a question for me to answer - she tags me in Asana. This works for me because my groups are relatively small and I don't get asked questions every day. You might have a large Facebook group where it's popping off every hour and you need to be more reactive. That's great but remember the 20-minute impact these regular distractions will have on your daily productivity. Can you set some rules around the time when you will go into your group to answer questions and engage? Can you guess what I'm going to suggest next? Time track how long you spend in your groups engaging and answering questions. Maybe you need to outsource some of this to a community manager so you can focus on the bigger picture work.

Social Media tasks your VA can do for you:

1. Create images
2. Create captions from your long-form content
3. Schedule posts
4. Reply to comments
5. Follow ideal clients
6. Manage Facebook group join requests
7. Add people to your email list when they opt in via socials
8. Notify you when you're asked a question
9. Block spammers

Can you afford to outsource yet?

I've just tasked you with a new way of creating content that might feel like it's more work than just creating a few Social Media posts each month. Write an entire blog? Record a podcast or video? I don't have time for that! I hear you cry. You absolutely do have time once you stop spending so much of it on Social Media or being distracted and now we're going to look at freeing up even more of time by considering what you might delegate and outsource in your business. Before you skip ahead because you don't have the budget to hire someone, hear me out. This is the classic trap I see a lot of solopreneurs staying stuck in: doing all the things because they can't afford to delegate. I'd argue that you don't have the budget to outsource because you are working too hard on tasks that don't bring money into your business. Something has to change.

Let's do a quick stock take of your time:

1. Write a list of everything you currently do in your business. From bookkeeping, to design, to copywriting, to delivering the client work
2. Against each item, mark with a single £ if this is a low-skilled task (such as designing Social Media posts in Canva, managing your diary, uploading videos, manually adding subscribers to your email list, creating invoices or sending out contracts etcetera)
3. Mark with ££ if this is a medium-skilled task (such as web design, bookkeeping, some elements of sales, designing marketing collateral or setting up email automations etcetera)

4. Mark with £££ if this is a highly-skilled task (such as copywriting and anything that truly ONLY you can do - like meet with clients and deliver the highly skilled parts of their work)

When it comes to outsourcing and delegating, begin with the tasks marked with a single £. Generally, these are the jobs a great assistant can do for you.

Pro tip: if you are resisting delegating these tasks because they only take a minute or two - you still need to stop doing them yourself because all those minutes add up! You might believe it will take you longer to explain to someone else how to do it than continuing to do it yourself. This isn't true. You can record yourself doing the task once, delegate it by sharing the video with your new assistant and you'll never have to do it again. It's one less thing to think about and all those little jobs have been cluttering up your mind and adding to feeling overwhelmed. It's time to breathe a sigh of relief that you have taken care of the small things. You have bigger fish to fry - money-making fish! An added bonus of delegating £ tasks is your position in your business becomes elevated. It's a whole new vibe when you no longer do your own admin and you can ride this next level feeling straight to your next goal.

You don't need to hire an employee - there are amazing freelancers who will come into your business on an hourly rate or to complete a specific project. I hired a VA in August 2020. If you recall from Chapter One, this was my worst financial month to date in my fledgling business because I'd let go of most of my clients. It was a huge point of change for me as I knew that by having a VA do all the £ jobs I had been doing up to that point was going to free up my time and head-space to both market myself to better clients and create a group programme that I would launch just one month later. My VA started on two hours a week and she's still with me three years later. I never regretted taking the time to show her how to upload videos into my group programme or how I like my Instagram feed to look. It was time well spent because it's saved me hours and hours in the long term.

To find the right person to support your business simply look at where your strengths and weaknesses lie. What tasks do you really dislike doing? What do you struggle with the most? I'm great with words but struggle with visual design so I knew I needed a VA who was good with Canva and had an eye for design. Write up your wish list and ask your network for recommendations.

Since hiring my VA I also got an accountant. The first time I had to do my tax return was time-consuming and super stressful for me (what if I get it wrong?). I asked my local network for recommendations, had a meeting and hired her. My accountant does all my bookkeeping and tax returns and as I've since gone limited, she set all of that up and now does my VAT returns too. There was no way I had the time or expertise to figure out how to do all of those things. For a relatively low fee each month, I know that my accounts are in order. I can turn my attention to bringing in the money instead of doing the admin around it.

Your next step is to complete the quick stock take of your time, noting what you are doing across the three different values of tasks in your business (£, ££ and £££).

Chapter 5

Why Positive Psychology?

In Chapter Three I shared a Positive Psychology intervention called Red and Green activities and explained how you can use strengths psychology to bolster your energy when faced with tasks that drain you. Now it's time to look at Positive Emotions and how emotions affect your productivity and ability to show up as the person you want to be in both life and business.

Positive Emotions

There were two statistics from the Positive Psychology scientific research I learned about during my studies that simultaneously blew my mind and made me feel super excited to put into action.

The first was:

50% of our emotions are pre-determined by our genetics. This is your base point and explains why some people seem naturally happier than others. It has been scientifically proven that only 10% of our emotions are affected by our circumstances and situations. Leaving a massive 40% of our emotions being within our control.

Read that again: 40% of how positive we feel every day is down to us. This is a huge opportunity to feel better.

I'd like to clarify what is classed as a Positive Emotion because I'm not referring to toxic positivity where you stick a smile on and pretend everything is OK. As an introduction to understanding positivity, I love this list of Positive Emotions by Professor Barbara Frederickson:

1. Inspiration
2. Interest
3. Awe
4. Joy
5. Amusement
6. Pride
7. Hope

8. Gratitude
9. Serenity
10. Love

If you did the VIA Character survey referenced in Chapter Two, you might notice some crossover with the emotions described here and the list of twenty-four character strengths. In my VIA report I am high in Hope and Gratitude and when I can bring these emotions into play using my strengths then I feel my sense of well-being surge.

If you are naturally pessimistic or experience negative emotions frequently you can train yourself to become more positive. You have the power within that 40% to shift your mood and outlook on life. When I learned this, I felt so excited to share this with everyone I know - I'm so glad I get to share this good news with you too.

Now onto the second piece of research that gave me a determination to utilise Positive Psychology in my business:

20-30% of business performance is determined by people's moods.

Positivity increases your chance of success as you're much more likely to feel motivated when you have a positive mindset and mood.

Would you like to boost your business performance by 20-30% and increase the chance of your business succeeding? Is that a "hell yes"? It was for me! I'll now explain how you can get started on experiencing more Positive Emotions more frequently.

How to start prioritising yourself and boosting your positivity

If you're so deep in the trenches of working in and on your business, you may have lost sight of some of the benefits that come with being your own boss. I bet these perks were something you were excited to experience once you decided to do your own thing - especially if you came to entrepreneurship from working a nine to five or shift work.

Cast your mind back to when you first decided to start your own business.

- What did you imagine your self-employed life would look like?
- Did you envision much more free time to dedicate to your hobbies or for relaxation?

- Did you start a business so you can spend more time with your family?
- Maybe you walked away from the corporate life or shift work because it was taking too much from you and you craved a more flexible way of working.

For me, I left my marketing manager job with one clear goal in mind: by the time my daughter enrolled in infant school I'd be available to walk her to and from school every day and be at home with her during the holidays. This was all I wanted and I'll never take for granted the lifestyle that I've created for us where I get to do this. It's a privilege a lot of parents don't have. My gratitude strength comes into play when I reflect on this perk of being self-employed!

To help you get back to feeling excitement every day about the potential your business affords you to live life on your terms, I invite you to try an exercise proven to positively influence the 40% of your emotions that are within your control. Ready for a boost?

Positivity Boosters Activity

Take ten minutes to yourself to do this exercise. You'll need something to take notes on.

Step one:

Think about the things that have made you happy In the last month. Write down anything that makes you laugh or smile. These can be small things that you do on a daily basis or bigger experiences.

You might struggle to list much at first; especially if you are stressed or very busy. Know that you can list simple pleasures like a good cup of coffee or listening to the sound of rain on the window.

Refer back to Professor Frederickson's list of ten Positive Emotions if you are struggling to think of things that give a jolt of happiness or joy. Positivity can also come from feelings of serenity and love. It might help you to add to your list by walking through your day hour by hour and note down anything that made you feel happy or a Positive Emotion from the list.

The key to this exercise is to write down everything that comes to mind; regardless how big or small. Don't leave things off the list because they seem insignificant to you or perhaps don't sound as exciting as a holiday to the Maldives. You should also include anything that you love doing or want to experience more often; think hobbies, exercise or even things you were good at as a child but have fallen by the wayside. *This has reminded me that I loved to roller skate as a teenager!*

Jot down activities you enjoy but haven't done for a long time. Consider the people whose company you enjoy and make you feel great when you're around them. Maybe you haven't seen a good friend or family member recently. Even better if there's someone in your life who makes you belly laugh! Put all of these people and activities on the list. It doesn't matter if you don't have a lot of good friends or family in your life; you are doing great if there is just one person who makes you feel good. Write their name down and take a moment to feel grateful for them.

To show you how the small things in life can absolutely count towards inducing positivity in your life I'll share ten of my 'happy things' with you here (it's OK if you don't have ten or if you have more - try and write as many as you can):

1. Going for a coffee and cake with Penny after a visit to the library. We munch our treats and flick through our books together
2. Swimming on a Monday afternoon, followed by the sauna
3. Sitting in the early morning sunshine to do a short meditation before I start the day
4. Chatting with my school mum friends in the playground
5. Banter with Adam while watching TV together after Penny has gone to bed
6. Kitchen dancing with Penny to Kisstory bangers on the radio
7. Playing loud music in the car
8. Hunting in the charity shop for bargain books with Penny
9. Going to see my mum and stepdad, dad and stepmum for a cup of tea and a chat
10. Reminiscing on fun times with my best friend (ideally over a cocktail)

Step two:

Think of points of your day, week, month where you can add some of the things you enjoy into your life. Ideally these will become more of a regular feature in your life and to achieve this it can help to tie them to your routine. Here's an example:

Driving to the office: Play your favourite songs in the car nice and loud! Extra positivity points for singing along.

Lunchtime: Go for a walk around the block, aiming to find some nice trees to look at because being around nature gives us a mood boost.

Bedtime: Light a scented candle and curl up in bed with a good book.

These are all simple pleasures and they are activities that I make sure to add into my week as often as I can. I pay extra attention to carving out time for them when work feels busy or stressful. If you end up talking yourself out of making time for the good things in your life then remember that by boosting your Positive Emotions you can harness an extra 20-30% of productivity! It pays to take that midday walk or go to bed early with your book.

I know from experience that it's easy to put this list away somewhere and forget to look at it. I recommend pinning it somewhere where you will see it often and make the commitment to start small by doing just one thing a week from your list; build up to adding the boosters into three points of your daily routine as per the guide above. Put the activity in your calendar and reflect how you feel at the end of the day when you've made the time for a positivity booster.

A further recommended use for your list of Positivity Boosters is to attach them to a task that you don't enjoy or something which induces negative emotions for you. Consult your list of red activities from Chapter Three.

An example of attaching a positivity booster to a red task in my business:

When tackling a big copywriting project that feels creatively tiring, I work on it in the gym cafe immediately after a sweaty workout. The exercise endorphins boost me through the task.

Attaching a positivity booster to a task or experience that you don't enjoy or find tedious is called habit stacking and it can be a game-changer for your ability to get things done with more enjoyment and to a higher standard.

The Every Day Holiday

Now that I've introduced you to Positivity Boosters, hopefully you feel inspired to add these into your routine and use them as you need them. But it doesn't stop there! Remember, we have 40% of our emotions within our control and the more positive we feel then the more productive we are. We also affect the positivity of people around us; imagine a ripple effect where when we feel good we can lift others up too.

I would love for you to go to the next level with your personal happiness and positive vibes so that you feel as good as you possibly can every single day. One of the ways I do this on top of habit stacking is to take an 'Every Day Holiday'. I didn't coin the phrase, credit goes to Dr Rangan Chatergee and his brilliant podcast *Feel Better, Live More*. In the podcast Dr Chatergee talks about taking time out for yourself every day and doing something that you perhaps reserve exclusively for holidays or time off from work. As an example, I know a lot of people who only read fiction when they are on holiday by the beach or the pool. When I listened to Dr Chattergee describe this concept I realised this is what I have been doing thanks to Positive Psychology and I see how this daily happiness boost affects my success. I do something small for myself every day that makes me feel good and I know this has a significant impact on reducing my stress levels and increasing my sense of overall well-being.

A simple example of how I put this into action is reading for pleasure. I was a real bookworm as a child and these days reading gives me the sense of escaping any worries from the day. When I first created my list of Positivity Boosters I recognised the role that reading plays in my overall happiness, inner peace, and I've baked reading into my routine most days now. I've carved out time for daily reading by making the effort to be in bed by 10 p.m. so I have time to read a chapter or two before I go to sleep. For me, I know that reading for half an hour is more beneficial than watching another episode of something on Netflix and going to bed later.

My next level holiday-style reading comes when I set my alarm an hour early, sneak downstairs to make a cup of tea, and in the summer months I sit outside and read with the birds chirping all around me. If it's cold outside, I take my cuppa back up to bed and snuggle down with my book. Such a gorgeous, relaxed way to start the day. At least, it's gorgeous and relaxed if my tea brewing doesn't wake Penny up! I don't have a 100% success rate with early morning reading.

Look at your own routine and ask yourself:

- When might you be able to take some time for yourself before you start work for the day?
- If you're a parent then perhaps you can find time after the school run or before you leave the house for wherever you'll be working that day.
- With or without kids, can you pause and take some time for yourself as a mini reset after the rush of leaving the house?

My favourite Every Day Holiday activity is sweating it out in the sauna. My gym has both a sauna and a steam room and I'm a regular at both. Adding fifteen minutes to sit in the heat after my workout makes me feel incredible and like I've made it in life! The positive effect the sauna has on my mood is even greater if I'm the only person in there because it's mid afternoon on a Tuesday and everyone else is at work. The feeling I get from treating myself to some relaxation time gives me the energy to make the most of the time I'm at work that week. It's the 20-30% productivity boost in action.

Here are some others of my favourite Every Day Holiday activities to inspire creation of your own:

- Taking my book to the park on during lunch
- Treating myself to a solo coffee at a coffee shop and half an hour to read my book
- Going swimming (then sauna!)
- Yoga class (then sauna!)
- Doing a face mask
- Getting a massage or manicure
- Meeting my friends for dinner
- Going to the twilight spa with Adam after work

You don't have to go on holiday to feel like you've had a break. The reason I'm sharing this concept of taking small pockets of time for yourself is because so many of us rush from task to task and hurry to complete all of our chores and meet the demands of everyone asking for something from us we don't take just a few minutes to do something we enjoy. It's a sad state of affairs and one that I hope this Chapter has shone a light on for you.

What can you do TODAY for yourself? Pick one small thing and give yourself a mini holiday wherever you are. You'll feel so much better for it.

Chapter 6

Your revenue-generating tasks

One of the key ways I grew my business from £2k-£3k months as a freelancer to a six-figure turnover by myself and only working twenty hours a week, was by prioritising the projects that would bring in future money on a bigger scale and diversifying my revenue streams. I maxed out at 'done for you' marketing projects and retainers pretty early on. I needed an alternative way to make more money as there weren't enough hours in the day to take on more clients. My new revenue streams away from 1-1 client work included group programmes where I teach marketing; new 'done with you' mentoring services. I also took time and consideration to tweak my 1-1 packages to ensure the profit margin increased alongside my expertise and the results my clients were getting.

In the first six months of my business, I was too busy with client work and trying to figure out how to run a business to look at making big changes and testing new offers. I didn't have enough data to understand what was working or what I really enjoyed doing. I feel this is a right of passage for every new business owner. You'd be a unicorn if you started a business and straight away had everything figured out and anyway, for most of us, we don't really know what's possible for our business until we've been running it for a while.

Most service-based solopreneurs go through a phase where they don't charge enough and it takes trial and error over time to work out how to make money with relative ease. The majority of us also start from zero in terms of audience size and email list, having to rely on referrals from our existing network which can make things even harder when your new business is not related to your previous career. You can cut yourself some slack if you're still in your first year of business and you feel like you're stuck on a hamster wheel of trading time for money and you can't see the wood for the trees in terms of how you'll scale what you've currently got. If this is you then read this Chapter knowing that you can start to implement these tips and strategies now to make your work life feel easier and ultimately free up the creative head-space with more time in the day to make changes to your business based on the results you're getting.

If you've been in business for over twelve months and you've completely plateaued or you're tired out, not loving it and you're trapped in a cycle of feast and famine revenue then it's time to take back control of your time and make changes to your business. There's only so long you can put up with working long hours for not enough financial reward or fulfilment before you decide to quit and go back to work for the Man. Let's not get to that point!

If you want to make changes to your business model and offers, pivot to serve a different ideal customer, free up the time to implement new marketing strategies or do something creative like write a book about your area of expertise then the time won't magically appear for you. It's up to you to make it happen. In Chapter Three we looked at how you can get more time back by creating boundaries around screen time and Social Media usage and I shared my spin on the Pomodoro Technique. You're now ready for next level productivity!

I need to dish out some tough love before we get into the 'how to' of getting more done in your business.

The truth is that YOU have created the business that you have and it's up to you to change it if it isn't serving you. How you choose to spend your working hours isn't down to anyone else, because ultimately, you are in charge of your time. You don't have a boss telling you what to do and when it needs to be done by. You are in charge and this is still the case even if you have demanding clients or family responsibilities pulling you from pillar to post. It's your choice on how to balance the demands on your time and only you can decide to make the necessary changes to move your business forwards. But I get that it can feel impossible to carve out the time for anything else when you're in the middle of it all and you're tired. Therefore, we are going to start with the basics which will allow you to make informed changes to your schedule. We're going to start with tracking your time.

Where does all your time go?

If you don't know where your time goes then you can't make changes to free up some of it which makes it tricky to estimate how much time you need to allocate to particular projects or tasks. If your goal is to work fewer hours then you need to understand what you currently spend your time working on.

- How much time are you spending on client work?
- How much time on your own marketing?
- How much time on admin?

I recommend using a free time tracking tool called Toggl: www.toggl.com to find out

I used Toggl in my previous life as a marketing manager, as did the entire business I worked for. It was invaluable for understanding how much resource we put into marketing and sales. This came in handy as I prepared to go on maternity leave as we had all the data to understand how much human resource we would need to cover my projects. It was a natural transition for me to use Toggl when I started my own business because not only did I want to have an overview of how long I was spending working for each of my clients, I also wanted to make sure I was dedicating enough time to working ON my business to move it forward. If you've never tracked your time before, I promise this will be a revelation! I also find there's a bonus side effect of seeing the Toggl timer ticking away on a project which means you're less likely to want to procrastinate on it.

You're going to need categories to track your time. Here's my recommendation on the types of Projects you might require to set up in Toggl to log all the different kinds of work that you do:

1. **Clients**: Each client will have their own project to record time against
2. **Marketing:** Such as copywriting, updating your website, posting on Social Media
3. **Prospecting** Such as sales calls, managing your spreadsheet of leads, chatting to leads in the DMs
4. **Admin** Such as emails, invoicing, contracts
5. **Personal development** This could be coaching or time spent learning a new skill
6. **Bespoke projects** For bigger one-off tasks such as the time I spent creating my email marketing programme

Optional extra could be adding another layer of data in Toggl by using Tags under each project. Such as when tracking time against a client I would use a tag to show it was for a 'Meeting' or 'Copywriting'.

I recommend tracking your time for thirty days to achieve a clear picture of how you are spending it at work. Keep tracking indefinitely because as your business evolves you'll be able to refer to this data to make informed decisions about how you use your time to make money and what resources you might need as you grow.

Making more money in less time

Once you are armed with some data about how you are spending your working hours then you can analyse it to work out which activities are most profitable for you or which ones aren't delivering the revenue as you hoped they would. Simply divide the money received by the hours spent on the job and you'll have your hourly rate in black and white. You might have started your business with a desired hourly rate in mind meaning you can use these figures to work out if your client work is profitable enough for you.

If you're brand new to running your own business and you've worked out an hourly rate then I have some advice for you: remember that your hourly rate doesn't only need to cover the time spent working for your client. It also includes the time you spend on everything else you do in your business such as admin and marketing. Don't forget that the tax office will be taking a cut and you'll need to pay into a pension as well.

Once you know exactly how much cash your projects are generating then you can start to make decisions to do less of the tasks that bring in the lowest hourly rate and more of the work that brings in the most revenue for the least amount of time spent working.

Here are some questions to answer as you assess your workload and the money you are bringing in:

- What type of client work is most profitable for you in terms of hourly rate once you divide how much you charge by the hours spent working?
- What type of work is quick for you to do?
- What type of work feels enjoyable?
- What type of work takes a long time?
- What type of work feels draining?

It's important to look at how easy work feels for you because there is also a cost in terms of the energy you pour into your clients and business. In the first six months of running my business, time tracking helped me to see that I was undercharging for most of my clients. Projects were taking longer than I'd estimated and I was working for way less than I was comfortable. My Toggl data helped me to decide which contracts to end, the type of work to say "no" to in the future and crucially, where the easy money was for me.

It's perfectly OK to embark on time-consuming projects if you enjoy the work and are paid well for it. It's the client work that runs over schedule and makes you feel overworked and resentful that needs to go ASAP. I know this can feel scary because it's money coming in after all, but if all of your time and energy is tied up in low-paid, draining work then you won't be able to make the necessary changes to bring in better, higher-paying clients or diversify your revenue streams. It might be worth a short-term financial hit for longer-term prosperity and fulfilment.

When it comes to the back end of your business, time tracking will give you the insights you need to delegate or even eliminate certain tasks. I looked at everything I was tracking as 'Admin' and used this to help me decide what to give to my virtual assistant. I could also see how much time tagged as 'Design' as part of my marketing and decided I would hire a VA who could take on design work. My hourly rate is way too high for me to spend making things look pretty in Canva! My zone of genius is copywriting and creating new income streams for my business so the more time I have available for this, the more money I can bring in. Get clear on what you should be doing in your business and what you should outsource.

Through my monthly Toggl reports I began to see a correlation between how much marketing and prospecting I was doing and how much money I was invoicing each month. If I had a month that was light on the marketing and sales activity, I saw a negative impact on my revenue over the next month. My time tracking has shown me that the sweet spot in my business for bringing in consistent revenue comes from dedicating one third of my time every month to my own marketing.

Take a look at how much time you're spending on marketing your business. If you are spending less than 20% of your time on marketing, I suspect you'll have a problem with consistent lead generation and your sales pipeline. If marketing isn't something you have much experience in, it's smart to get some expert advice on this because without marketing, you don't have your business set up for success. When you have it dialled in, your marketing and sales process is how you attract and convert clients on a consistent basis.

Put your own work first because clients can wait (gasp!)

Now that you know what you are spending your time on every day, week and month, you can start to become more intentional about how you structure your working week. If you've discovered that you aren't dedicating enough time to marketing your business then I recommend putting blocks of time into your calendar BEFORE you schedule in time for clients. This might feel like a radical (or even impossible) suggestion because, of course, clients are paying you and you have deadlines to meet. However, if you're serious about wanting to make changes to your business then you need to dedicate the time to make these changes. The best way that I've found to do this is to put blocks of time into my calendar in the morning to work on my own marketing, content creation and bigger project work that is essential to generating future revenue. Client work can absolutely be scheduled for afternoons or on certain days I'll block out most of the day for a client's project so that I can get into flow with it and complete the task efficiently.

Look at how your working week is currently structured (or not!) and if you are bouncing from client to client, project to project or task to task then you will likely feel like you don't have the focus you need to really break the back of any given piece of work. This is a terrible way to work because your brain is constantly having to catch up and try to get in the zone with multiple ideas. To bring efficiency into your working week, we'll now look at time blocking.

How to time block like a pro

If you've tried time blocking before and it didn't work out for you, I'd like you to give it another go by doing it my way. The key to successful time-blocking is reviewing your time blocks at the end of every day and you're allowed to shuffle things around as you go. Over the past three and a half years of managing the time I have available to work on my business I've experienced a multitude of interruptions and curveballs that life throws at us all from time to time. To be able to flex and bounce back from a scheduling setback you will need to adopt a somewhat fluid approach to your timetable so that when your cat has to go to the vet, you get ill, your kid is unexpectedly off school then your meticulously planned calendar doesn't go up in flames.

Here are my recommendations for time blocking and the rules I operate my schedule by:

- Put “me time” aka your Every Day Holiday (see Chapter Five) in your calendar FIRST. All of my gym classes, dinner dates, massages etcetera are in my diary in purple. If I don’t see any purple then I know it’s all work and no play and I’m going to have a bad month.
- Put in at least thirty minutes for lunch every day. I always start with forty-five minutes but if I’m struggling to fit in calls I’ll shorten it to thirty.
- Put in family or child commitments and quality time activities. These are yellow in my diary and ensure I never forget a swimming lesson, school library trip or these days - a teacher strike day.
- Block out one day a week for no calls. No-calls days (Fridays) are red in my diary and my VA knows not to book anything in on those days.
- School holidays and family holidays are blocked out in orange.

Now that all the personal non-negotiables are in, add in calls.

- I put in forty-five-minute blocks for my 1-1 client calls and one-hour blocks for any group programme calls. These calls are light green and are allocated to clients as we go through the month.
- I make sure any calls with my mentor or coaches are in the diary in blue.
- My VA adds in any guest training sessions or podcast interviews I'm doing. These are light purple in my diary and I aim to do at least one every week to grow my audience.
- When I'm in sales mode, I allocate up to a dozen thirty-minute discovery calls slots in my diary for the week. These are dark green.

That's all my calls in the diary for the month. Now it's time to add in blocks of time to do some project work. These blocks are pink in my calendar. I use Asana for my project management, so I'll consult this to see what work is on my 'to do' list and what deadlines are coming up.

- I block a maximum of two hours for work that requires deep levels of concentration. Cal Newport's book, *Deep Work*, recommends doing focussed work for a maximum of ninety-minute stretches with ninety minutes rest; that we are capable of focussing on tasks that require high levels of concentration for just four hours each day. I don't have enough unbroken time in the day for two ninety-minute blocks with ninety minutes in between, but I know from experience that two hours is enough for me to make headway with a task that requires high levels of concentration. Something for you to bear in mind as you plan in your focussed work.

- I schedule one hour each week to write my email newsletter. If I'm planning a blog that week, I put in ninety minutes to get it written.
- Client work goes in around everything else!
- Writing this book was originally scheduled for early mornings, Fridays and weekends. I eventually found it was more efficient to binge-write the bulk of it over a two-week period instead of my original plan to write in small batches over several months. I couldn't keep my train of thought intact when trying to write it over many weeks and it became less efficient than expected. It was an intense couple of weeks writing most of the book in such a short space of time and I had to sacrifice some family time to get it written. I was comfortable with the trade off because I

have always wanted to write a book and I completed it in time for the school summer holidays. Phew!

Finding the time to create and launch new offers

Thus far you know how to find out which clients and projects are making you the most money in the least amount of time and you've overhauled your calendar to become a colour-coded balance of work, restoration and quality time with loved ones. But there's still one big problem we haven't addressed: you don't actually have the time to get everything done. Same here! This is how we're going to handle that.

Sunday night planning and your daily review

Alongside my rainbow Google calendar system, I use Asana to keep track of my mammoth 'to do' list, client work or anything else I don't want to forget. I recommend using a tool like Asana, Trello or Notion (there are dozens available) to house all of your ideas and tasks. Every Sunday evening, I spend fifteen minutes consulting Asana to see which tasks have deadlines coming up and then check my Google calendar for space to insert pink blocks of time to do this work. Every week, without fail, I have more work to do than there are hours available. This realisation makes me feel positive because I've recognised it ahead of time, rather than a deadline popping up that I'd forgotten about and causing me a lot of stress.

Sunday night planning forces me to make a choice on what to prioritise and no, not everything can be labelled a priority. At this point I look at the list of tasks due that week and make some calculated decisions to delegate, eliminate or bump the task to another date. Planning my week ahead this way was one of the reasons I invested in a VA so early on in my business. There were admin and routine tasks that needed completing and I couldn't keep doing them myself because the bigger projects for the future success of my business kept getting delayed. They had to be outsourced or I was going to fail at running my business.

Some questions to ask as you review your 'to do' list and available working hours:

- If a task hasn't been started in the last six months, is it really that important? Can you eliminate it?

- Does it need to be YOU doing all of these tasks? What could you outsource?
- Which tasks will result in revenue coming into your business this month or next? Make time for those!
- What tasks can be moved to next week to give you the head-space to get started on, or complete, the revenue-generating tasks this week?

Focus on Monday morning

The benefit of getting a head start on planning your week ahead is that when you sit down to work on Monday, you know exactly what you're going to be doing. There's no time wasted trying to figure out what to do first or dropping straight into overwhelm. You've already worked out that you don't have time to do everything and you've chosen a task to kick off the week because it's important to get done.

A word of warning: do not derail your best laid plans for the week by starting your working day with opening your inbox! As soon as you check your emails, you're adding to the mental load with a bunch of requests on your time and limited resource. If you run your working day by responding to emails as they come in, you are allowing other people to take charge of your time and your 'to do' list. The same goes for messages and voicemails. Choose a strategic time to check in with your inbox and messages. The best time to do this is not the first half of your day. For me, I wait until mid-morning at the very earliest to check messages and emails.

How to prevent email from ruling your life

If my recommendation to leave checking your emails until later in the day brought you out in a cold sweat, it's worth taking some time right now to consider a new way of handling your communications with clients, suppliers and other stakeholders. For me, I use email at the bare minimum in my business. I currently have one retainer client who communicates with me on email. I've set the expectation that I don't respond immediately. We have a short catch up call once a week and I tend to answer all the queries that come in on email during that call. Guess what happens if I reply to emails? I get more email replies with more actions or questions! This isn't an efficient way for anyone to work, in my experience.

Here's a bonus tip for you: use your email software scheduling tool to send replies when you want the recipient to receive them. For me, I tend to batch respond to emails late in the day and I don't want replies coming back to me out of office hours because often that will create the expectation I'll respond because I'm online. I use Gmail and I'll schedule most of my email replies to go at 9 a.m. the next day. If you don't want your clients to know you're online during evenings or weekends, use the scheduling tool and it removes the impression that you work outside of normal office hours and will therefore reply out of hours.

For all of my 1-1 clients we use Voxer to send text messages and voice notes, I set up a shared Google Drive folder to access documents we're collaborating on. My clients don't email me and I don't email them. It's beautiful. Of course, you can end up replacing the email workload with an instant messenger workload so you need to let your clients know what the expectations are for receiving replies. My contract states my turnaround time for replying to messages and it's certainly not instantly or during evenings and weekends. I love voice notes because I can listen on the move or while taking a break from sitting at my desk. I also play them at double speed sometimes!

Voice notes can certainly replace the need for frequent meetings or phone calls. I use them for sending ideas back and forth with a client and they're a great way to celebrate their progress. My clients and I can land on making key decisions way quicker over Voxer than on email.

Here is your key takeaway and reflection on your use of email: if you run your working day from your inbox, you are letting other people decide on your focus and dictate how you spend your time that day. Are you OK with that?

When are you most productive?

You likely have an idea of whether you're a morning person or a night owl when it comes to being productive. I'm definitely quicker at copywriting during the morning. Therefore, I'll block mornings for creative writing projects. I prefer to do calls in the afternoon where possible or even batch client calls for a day where I know that's my sole focus and all that's expected of me is to show up with my ideas and energy.

When you're putting in your time blocks on a Sunday night choose the best time of day for you to complete the task at hand efficiently. In Chapter Three we looked at red and green activities and your energy levels. Be mindful of this as you map out your working week.

Batching to get the job done

Another productivity hack you can add to the toolkit you're building is batching. I do this for content creation because I know that when I get in the zone with a creative idea I can keep going at it until it's done. If I don't have enough time on one day to complete a creative task then I try to organise the next day so that I pick it up again straight away, or I'll set my alarm for 6 a.m. and get it finished while it's still fresh in my mind. Do whatever you need to do with the time you have available to get it done.

I used batching to plan, write, build and launch my first ever pre-recorded group programme (Electric Email). This is a perfect example of putting in focussed time and creative energy to launch a new revenue stream. When I looked at everything I needed to create to make a self-paced course live, it felt like a huge project. It was certainly a significant piece of work but as with anything, it could be broken down into its component parts and batched to delivery.

Here's how I planned, batch created and launched a brand new online programme (still only working twenty hours a week):

1. I mapped out what I needed to teach my ideal clients to get them to their desired result and split this into three main parts of the course (the modules)
2. For each module I listed out every topic and subtopic I would need to teach to get them to their desired result
3. I decided to script each lesson to make it as punchy and actionable as possible
4. I batch wrote the lesson scripts over a couple of weeks. Mostly I worked from Costa to do this because it was just before I got my new office space and my kitchen table wasn't inspiring me to get the work done.
5. I batched the written content for supporting workbooks and resources and passed these to my VA to design into PDFs
6. I batch recorded all the lessons over the space of three days. I had my new office by this point and so I could go in and be uninterrupted while recording.
7. I batch uploaded all of the finished content into the members area in Kartra

8. I batched the sales email copywriting and building the launch email sequence in Kartra

From concept to finished course, I clocked up sixty hours in Toggl. If I had tried to find sixty hours in one go in my calendar I would have said that it was impossible. In fact, I carved out the time over a matter of a few weeks to get this created and launched because I knew I could batch a lot of it and I was motivated to test out a self-paced programme. At the time, I was fully booked for 1-1s and I wanted somewhere to send clients to give them the result they wanted, to get their email marketing working.

The result of my focussed work was having my first £10,000 month just fifteen months into running a business. That course went on to bring in multiple tens of thousands of pounds for my business. I think this is a pretty epic result for a one-woman band and her VA.

You can create anything you want to in your business when you map out the individual elements and put the time into your calendar. Otherwise, it's just an idea or a dream.

Chapter 7

Slowing down time

Since becoming a mum, I've become hyper-aware of time in the sense I feel more keenly the minutes and hours passing by. I think this is the result of the complete lifestyle change; from having all the time in the world to binge watch Netflix series, go mountain biking in the Peak District to living by a feeding-and-sleep schedule that left little space to even make myself a sandwich, never mind anything else.

If you're a parent, you'll know that once the newborn days are behind you there's always a new developmental stage with its own specific challenges that consume hours of your time. Like weaning! Trying to work out how to fit in the painfully slow intake of food around milk feeds felt like getting anything else done was impossible. I was either feeding milk or mushy food or crawling around on the floor cleaning up all the splatter. By the time Penny was one I didn't own a single pair of jeans that still had knees in them. Luckily I like the punk rock look so I wore my holey jeans for a few years until my Weetabix removal days were over.

All that the time spent nurturing Penny has left an imprint on me which seems to have manifested into an aversion to wasting time. I'll be honest with you - this can cause problems at home and at work if I let it. The most startling symptom of my allergy to time-wasting shows up when we go away on holiday. Since starting my own business, I struggle to not think about or do work because I genuinely love it so much! Maybe in part because I only work twenty hours a week so I tend to think about work in other pockets of time when I'm not actually at my desk.

When I was employed I had no qualms about switching on my Out-Of-Office. If I was on holiday you didn't see or hear from me until I got back. I worked hard when I was in the office and I was determined I'd take proper time off to refresh and enjoy life; after all, that's why we go to work, right? To pay for holidays and the fun stuff! I don't view holiday time in exactly the same way as an entrepreneur because I'm so excited by the potential within my business that I want to be nurturing it all the time. I also have more time off from work anyway, so perhaps I'm not as in need of a holiday in order to get away from it all. It's great for me that I'm so into my business but not so great for the people who want to be around me without my laptop obscuring half of my face.

I'm much better these days now that I have a better awareness of the negative impact of taking work on holiday, but when I first started my business I didn't consider logging off completely for a week because I had so much stuff to do. This was partly because I was so busy wearing all the hats; I had no one to cover for me and I was undercharging and over delivering for my clients. The first time we went away as a family of three to Center Parcs for a week I took my laptop and actually did client work in Starbucks while Adam and Penny were doing pottery painting. I really regret this now! I wish I had painted a unicorn too...

Luckily I had my epiphany six months into running my business, burned it all down, hired a VA and committed to prioritising health and family more. This shift came about thanks to getting clarity on what I really want from life and business and discovering it wasn't taking my laptop to Center Parcs so I could work from a cafe.

With this new phase of enlightenment, I discovered a way to bend time and space to give me more hours in the day. Not literally more than twenty-four hours of course, but the effect of this new approach to viewing my use of time certainly makes it feel like I have more available to me. Would you like some more time too? Get ready because if you're also dragging your laptop around with you on holiday or feel like you're in a headless chicken mode far too often, I have a simple solution that will immediately help you feel like you can open up more time in your day.

There are two things that have helped me to benefit from the feeling of having more time to get stuff done. I discovered this first technique and the subsequent way to structure my weekly schedule after those first six months of thrashing myself in my business. The first practical technique for creating more time and space so that you feel less rushed and stressed is mindfulness. If you've tried mindfulness or meditation before and it's not your vibe - hear me out. You don't need to sit cross-legged in a flowy gown for ages. You can try various methods but before I share how you can do this, let's take a look at the science behind mindfulness and why you should adopt a practice for yourself.

In Positive Psychology, we work on creating Engagement as it's one of the six pillars in Professor Seligman's framework which contribute to living a meaningful and happy life. Facilitating Engagement through regularly using our strengths such as your green activities at work and your VIA Character Strengths. Getting into Flow Experiences and practising mindfulness gives us greater positive feelings and life satisfaction. There is a proven link between Engagement and Motivation and I want to help you feel as motivated as possible to reach your goals in the time you have available to you.

I didn't know about any of this when I started practising Mindfulness and Meditation. It was simply suggested to me as a way to help me connect with what I really wanted in life and my business because I had lost my way and was looking for guidance. When I dropped into a mindfulness practice and let go of my 'to do' list, I then asked myself some simple questions about what my ideal day and career looked like. From this I was able to clearly see that what I'd created in my business up to that point wasn't it. Meditation and slowing down my non-stop hustle-brain allowed me to practise reflection and gave me the head-space to experience a new clarity on the bigger vision for my business. This ultimately opened the way to making changes that helped me create a more fulfilling work-life integration.

Hopefully you're now curious enough to want to experience this for yourself and you've put aside whatever preconceptions you may have about mindfulness and meditation. Here's how you can start to benefit from the effects of mindfulness using a Positive Psychology intervention called Creating Quiet Time.

Creating Quiet Time Exercise

The aim of pausing and making space for nothing but sitting with yourself in silence is to help you to connect to your internal experiences, feelings and thoughts.

Becoming mindful of what's going on inside ourselves can be hard to do at first; especially in our busy lives and because we place so much attention on the things outside of ourselves –such as work and family.

You might find this practice uncomfortable at first because sitting in silence can show you what's going on in your internal world. I encourage you to stick with it because this is an essential tool to help you connect with yourself and ask questions about what you really want in life and your business. If you aren't clear on this, you'll ultimately waste even more time moving in the wrong direction or hustling your way through your holidays.

This exercise invites you to spend some time alone in silence this coming week. You can choose to spend anywhere from five minutes to an hour where you do nothing and simply be quiet. No music, podcasts, TV or phone. Just you. You can leave the house and go for a walk in silence if you prefer, just make sure you go to a quiet place.

Know it is normal for to you feel awkward at first! If you're anything like I was in the stressful early days of my business then you'll probably also want to make Quiet Time as short as possible because you have too much to do. You can start with just five minutes and build up. As you engage in quiet time more often, you may notice that you become more familiar and comfortable with silence. You may also begin to see how essential this time is for getting to know your internal world.

Here's your Quiet Time homework:

Step 1: Schedule in Quiet Time

Make a commitment to quiet time every day this week by scheduling this time in your diary.

Step 2: Post quiet reflection

After you complete your quiet time write about your experiences such as what feelings and emotions showed up, what thoughts passed through your mind and how you felt afterwards.

Step 3: Evaluation

At the end of the week ask yourself the following reflection questions:

- How did you find sitting in silence and being with yourself?
- Did you find it easy or difficult to integrate Quiet Time into your life?
- Will you continue to schedule in Quiet Time each week?

Here are a few ways I add Quiet Time into every day (I mix these up):

- I walk home from the school run without plugging into my headphones or checking my phone
- I set a timer for ten minutes and lay like a starfish on the bed, or on my office sofa, with my eyes closed.
- I do five minutes mindfulness after I've made my morning cuppa (if I'm up before the rest of the house)
- I do yoga calm class at the gym which is very quiet and includes fifteen minutes in Corpse Pose
- I sit in the sauna for fifteen minutes

Quiet time doesn't have to be the same every day. Make it different but stick to the principle of sitting in silence with only your internal thoughts and feelings for company.

Slowing down to speed up

I had my first lightbulb moment on what was important to me back in July 2020 as I sat in meditation mode followed by a guided visualisation about what I wanted my life and business to look like. I connected with an image of birds flying and my business soaring as I had even more time and space to spend with my loved ones and do creative pursuits away from work. I also wanted to go to the gym more because I knew how good it made me feel. These themes of time-freedom and space to nurture relationships, and my own health and wellness, come up for me again and again three years later and serves as a great reminder to stay on track with WHY I'm running my own business. If you can use quiet time to tune into your internal needs and desires; you too can start to uncover what you really want in life and business. After all, clarity on what's important to you is the first step to making changes.

When I was studying for my Positive Psychology coaching certification during the summer of 2022, I was on the receiving end of hours of coaching which helped me to explore what my mission and purpose in life is, what really makes me happy and what my version of success looks like. It turns out that it was much the same as in 2020 and it's still the same one year on as I write this. I want to:

- Be present for my friends and family
- Be healthy and physically fit
- Have time for creative pursuits outside of work
- Go on nice holidays (without my laptop)

The result of my ongoing inner work and self-reflection through Mindfulness and Visualisation is that I'm continually re-committing to scheduling in restoration time and gym sessions during the working day. This felt majorly uncomfortable to me back in 2020 because I was extremely busy with client work and trying to run and scale my business. I didn't have time to go for lunch walks or gym classes. This was also mid-pandemic and I'd only just managed to get Penny into childcare again, as nursery settings opened up, so it felt overindulgent to use some of my child-free time to NOT work. Here's how I eventually did it and how this became another way for me to open up what felt like more hours in the day.

I'd drop Penny off at nursery and go to the gym. I'd do my workout then get home to shower and start work. I was surprised to find that despite losing two hours in getting to the gym, doing the class, travelling home and having a wash, I didn't feel rushed for time. I'd sit down to work and I was getting tasks done to deadline with much less stress. I could close my laptop at the end of the day with a sense of accomplishment. I wondered what sort of time-bending magic was happening here? I had fewer hours available to work because I was scheduling in gym sessions yet I felt more productive, less rushed and more on it with my workload. It made no sense to my logical brain looking at the purple 'me time' taking up several hours in my short working week where previously there had been too many jobs vying for that precious block of time.

Three years on and I continue to surprise myself thanks to even shorter school days than the 8.30 a.m. - 5.30 p.m. nursery days of 2020. Today, with all the school holidays, I still manage to take time out of my short working day for non-work pursuits and feel on top of everything.

I have less time to work these days, but I get more done, what gives? The science of Positive Psychology can shed some light on this phenomenon. In Chapter Five, I shared with you that when we feel engaged and positive we are 20-30% more productive. I see the evidence of this in action for me. I come back from the gym and I'm on fire with my work. I feel positive and motivated to work not only thanks to post-workout endorphins but also because I feel so grateful that I've built a business that means I can go to a 9.30 a.m. gym class instead of the crazy busy 6 p.m. class (when I'm too tired anyway). I'm motivated to work to my full potential in the time I have available.

You don't need to go to the gym to experience the productivity benefits that come with boosting your Positive Emotions. Go back to your list of Positivity Boosters from Chapter Five and start allocating time for these in your busy schedule. You might resist doing this because you're so busy, but imagine if it does indeed work for you and as you start to allocate time to do the things that bring you joy, you experience the expansion of time and an uplift in productivity. Worth testing?

When overwhelm kicks in

I'm aware that you may be so overworked and stressed right now that you can't contemplate making space in your working day for yourself. If this is you, start with five minutes of quiet time every day and gradually increase this week-by-week, so, at the very least you are making some space to connect with yourself.

When overwhelm is taking over and stress is really impacting you, you have a stress-busting emergency toolkit you can use anytime: your breath. Your breath provides a direct signal to your autonomic nervous system which has two opposite functions. Take fast, shallow breaths and you begin to switch on the sympathetic nervous system, ready for fight or flight. When you slow down your breathing and focus on taking air deeper into the lungs, you activate the parasympathetic nervous system, or your mode of recovery and relaxation. We need both sympathetic and parasympathetic functions to survive, but we can get stuck in a sort of halfway mode between the two, never really being able to fully relax. This isn't healthy for our bodies long-term so it pays for your physical and mental well-being to learn a simple breathing technique that will activate your parasympathetic system to take you back to relaxation mode. A super easy breathing exercise called Box Breathing will provide a calming effect in just a few minutes.

Exercise: Box Breathing

This technique is used by Navy SEALs when they need to stay calm and focussed in stressful situations. If it works for them, it will definitely work for us when feeling stressed looking at our 'to do' list and unread emails. Here's how you do it:

- Inhale for a count of 4 seconds
- Hold for 4
- Exhale for 4
- Hold for 4
- Repeat at least 6 times (more if you need it)

If it helps you to keep track of the breaths, imagine your breath going along one of the four sides of a box for each count.

You can pause and do a few rounds of box breathing at multiple points in your day. I like to do it to ground myself before tackling certain projects or even after high-energy meetings to help me relax and concentrate for the next task at hand.

I've found that a positive side effect of regularly using Box Breathing is that I've become more aware of my breath in general. I realise when I'm taking shallow breaths because I'm rushing around and can immediately soften the belly and start to take air deeper into the lungs. Try it now! How are you currently breathing? Can you take the breath a little deeper and make it a little slower? How do you feel after focussing on the breath for a few inhales and exhales?

As part of my Positive Psychology studies, I read fairly extensively on the benefits of breath-work on the body and mind. It's fascinating to me that our breath has such a dramatic and immediate impact on our body and stress levels. If you're interested in learning more about using the breath to control stress then check out the teachings of Wim Hof. Wim uses a breathing technique to bring on stress via the sympathetic nervous system which over time allows more control over the physiological stress response. I also highly recommend the book *Breath - The New Science Of A Lost Art* by James Nestor. Fascinating stuff!

Chapter 8

Your new morning routine

When I first started following online business owners on Instagram in 2020 there seemed to be a trend around morning routines for success. My feed was full of enthusiastic female entrepreneurs waking up at 5 a.m. to drink a gallon of water, do exercise, journal, make a smoothie, meditate and then start work on their business by 8am.

At this point in time I had a three-year-old who would wake up if I tried to boil the kettle in the morning so it didn't seem feasible that I could implement a thorough morning routine for entrepreneurial success. It got to the point where I was so sick of Instagram showing me everyone's amazing candle-lit morning rituals that I had to unfollow a bunch of accounts because it made me feel like my lack of glossy routine was holding me back in some way. For two years of my new work life post 9-5 career I resisted any kind of morning ritual other than my usual rise, drink a glass of water, wash my face while the kettle boils, apply moisturiser while the tea brews then wrangle my child through breakfast, teeth brushing, getting dressed, putting shoes on etcetera before we could leave the house. I did the same thing every morning and it didn't involve any alone time or mental preparation for the day ahead. I was cool with that; morning routines just weren't for me.

Then, as part of my Positive Psychology training, I learned about Positivity Boosters and got curious about how I might implement a couple of these in the morning to give myself a really nice start to my day. I was finally open to testing out a new morning routine. I got it wrong to start with. I woke early, crept downstairs and ran through an epic twenty-minute ritual of breath-work, stretching, journaling, dancing around to a favourite song and then sitting with my eyes closed, visualising success. This was nice enough but after about ten days of doing it, it felt like too much. I had accidentally created a routine based on the glossy Insta-rituals of 2020 and it felt like a chore rather than a joyous start to the day. I'm sharing this with you because I'm about to recommend you add in a morning ritual to support your positivity and productivity, but I don't want you to think it has to be complicated and time-consuming. Unless you have the space to rise early and do multiple activities that make you feel good; if that's the case, go for it!

Why is it good practice to make a conscious effort to curate your waking moments? Because it sets you up for the day! If you rise and do something that makes you feel good first thing, you'll carry that energy throughout the morning and hopefully into the rest of the day. When we covered Positivity Boosters in Chapter Five, I shared how you can bake these into your daily routine around morning, midday and evening. If you identified a Positivity Booster you can seamlessly add into your morning routine, you already have the perfect addition to your day.

Struggling to decide what could constitute a morning ritual for you? Here's the quickest mini ritual to help you start the day in a positive way: gratitude practice. As you wake and roll out of bed, when your feet touch the floor, say "thank you" - out loud, if you can, for extra power! You are here for another day on Planet Earth and the simple practice of being grateful for that will give you a Positivity Boost. Begin to equate getting out of bed with being thankful and you will build a Positivity Habit to last a lifetime.

The science of gratitude

The science behind gratitude is compelling and I have to re-read it every so often to remind myself how powerful the results of these little actions can be. Being grateful is such a simple thing to do that it almost doesn't seem possible that it can have such a profound impact on our positive emotions.

What is gratitude? It's about focussing on the good, not the bad and being grateful for what we already have. So you can hopefully understand how starting the day with "thank you" instead of dreading something you aren't looking forward to doing, or dwelling on something bad that happened yesterday, you can create a simple shift from negative to positive right from the outset.

Some people are more naturally grateful - me for example! Gratitude is number two in my list of twenty-four VIA Character Strengths which means I feel fortunate and appreciative of the positive things in my life. If you aren't naturally high in gratitude, the good news is that it is a state you can get into regularly with practice. Why should you try to be more grateful for what you have? Well, on top of making you feel happier and therefore benefiting from that 20-30% productivity boost, years of research into gratitude interventions have shown it consistently produces:

- Better sleep
- Reduced fatigue
- Decreased depressed mood
- Improved cardiovascular health
- Higher belief in your ability to succeed
- Lower levels of inflammatory biomarkers
- Better adherence to medication, exercise and diet
- Reduced stress
- Improved positive self-evaluation
- Improved relationships

Gratitude costs nothing to practise and the benefits to both your mental and physical well-being are significant. Adding a moment of gratitude into your morning is an easy way to give yourself a boost before you get on with your day. No yoga mats or scented candles required.

Your flexible morning routine

If you are open to crafting a new morning routine that expands on the simple gratitude practice explained above, let's consider now what this might look like for you and what could work well for you in your current season of life.

My morning routine isn't very routine at all but the one common theme for every morning is that I take some time for myself. I know that when I do this, I feel like I've started the day on the right foot, which in turn makes me feel like I'm showing up as a great version of myself. It sets the tone for the entire day. I tend to change my morning routine based on the four seasons. For example, in winter, my favourite thing to do in the morning is creep out of bed before my family wakes, make a cup of Yorkshire Tea in my favourite china mug with the gold leaf patterns, carry it back up to bed and sip it while reading a fiction novel. Even better if it's dark and raining outside! I relish the cosiness and the indulgent feeling of doing something purely for pleasure and relaxation before I start my busy day. Now, this doesn't always go to plan because Penny might wake up and that means it's game over for novel reading. When this happens, I change the routine where she brings a book of her choice to my bed and I read it to her while I drink my tea. Still a lush, slow-paced way to start the day. I tie in gratitude with this as we cuddle up and enjoy that precious quality time together.

In the summer months, I've been known to take my cuppa out into the back garden and enjoy my book with a soundtrack of the birds going about their business in the trees at the bottom of the garden. I also enjoy listening to a morning meditation on the Insight Timer app whilst turning my face to the early morning sun. Bliss! If it's a little chilly out, I'll take a blanket and tuck it around me while I do the meditation.

I mentioned Wim Hof in Chapter Seven where I talked about the importance of the breath. I go through phases of doing Wim's eleven-minute free YouTube breath-work video in the morning. This is one you definitely need to do lying down or seated because it activates the sympathetic nervous system and can make you feel light-headed. I'll do this lying down under a blanket on the sofa, making sure to stretch and rise slowly once it's complete. I'm also a convert to cold showers thanks to learning about the Wim Hof Method but I don't enjoy the cold showers so much in the morning, instead I embrace the cold water in the evening and enjoy how warm my pyjamas then feel against my skin. This is also Mindfulness coming into play as the physical sensation of the cold water then the warm towel and pyjamas takes me away from my busy mind and helps me to focus on the present moment.

I've dabbled with morning visualisation where I'll pop my Airpods in, stick on a favourite song and imagine my best possible life. This involves my dream of living further out in the countryside and I have an amazing home office where I write books and have even more time than I do now to be creative.

The point I'm trying to make is: your morning routine can chop and change. You don't need to adhere to a rigid schedule or list of things you *must* do to have a fabulous day. If there's one thing I'd love for you to take from this chapter, it's making a more conscious decision over how you start your day. If you currently hit snooze over and over until dragging yourself out of bed at the latest possible moment and then have to hustle to be on time for your first appointment of the day, you only need to make small adjustments to how you wake up, to feel big benefits. As a snooze button user myself, my simple and super effective solution to repeatedly snoozing the alarm is to put it out of reach of my bed. I use my Apple Watch as an alarm and I place it on the dresser which is three steps away from my bed. I have to silence it quickly for fear of waking the child and therefore resigning myself to reading a kids' book instead of the latest Thursday Murder Club mystery. Once I'm up, I head to the bathroom to splash my face with cold water then I'm awake and not tempted to get back under the duvet. In reality, this takes about ten seconds of feeling uncomfortable for the reward of a morning's worth of positivity because I got up early, made my cuppa and did something nice for myself instead of dozing away that opportunity.

A note about your phone

At no point in these suggestions for your morning ritual have I suggested you pick up your phone to scroll Social Media, check your email or look at the news. Most people check their phone as soon as they wake up and if this is you, be warned that this habit can derail the best intentions to implement a new morning routine. It might be enough for you to set the boundary that you won't check your notifications until after your morning ritual is complete, but, if opening up that inbox or tapping on Instagram is too ingrained as a habit for you to wait until after breakfast then you might need to put in place a physical barrier.

I hold my hands up as I've mentioned already in this book that I had to uninstall certain Social Media apps and I even go as far as locking my phone in the boot of my car overnight to stop me from checking it - so I get it. It's an automatic response to open your phone first thing and deal with whatever has come in overnight. The problem with this is we can't control what we are going to be shown. It could be bad news, an email you feel pressured to respond to ASAP or a myriad of other people's opinions that can derail you from enjoying that first hour of the day. Whatever it is can wait until you've upped your positivity and thus resilience to tackle whatever the day (and your phone) throws at you.

Morning routine in holiday time

For the parents with school age kids reading this we'd better talk about morning routines in the school holidays because we have weeks of them interrupting our usual schedule. Of course, it depends on whether you are using kids' holiday clubs or childminders as to what your mornings look like in the holidays. I like to have Penny at home with me outside of term time, so we set our own routine. You can bet that on the first day with no school run, I'm having a lie in! In the summer holidays, Penny has her blackout blind up on her bedroom window and I pray to the sleep gods that she sleeps in later than her term time wake up call. If I naturally wake up before she does then cue the stealth kettle boiling and novel reading in bed before she's up.

As much as my business is built around taking it easy with work in school holidays, sometimes I do have work that I want or need to do. On those days I'll set my alarm an hour before I think Penny will wake up and creep into the living room with my laptop to get some stuff done. I also add in some mindfulness practice before and after working that early in the day. There's always a cup of Yorkshire Tea involved whether I'm working first thing or taking some time out before the busy day ahead. I think it's important for our sanity as parents to take some alone time where we can during the school holidays. It's intense and I don't know about you, but I'm definitely guilty of trying to make the most of this time off school, so I'll pack in day trips and play dates which can leave both of us pretty tired by the end of the first week!

Overall my simple aim, and I believe this should be your aim too, is to have a lovely start to the day. Recognise that if you need more sleep, take it, or if you're a repeat offender with the snooze button then take charge of the physical set up of your alarm and give yourself the gift of taking the time to indulge in something that makes you feel good before your diary commitments mean you don't get that chance. It might not look good on Instagram, my being in bed with my hair stuck up in a scrunchie, quietly sipping tea and turning pages while my husband sleeps beside me but it makes me feel way happier than when I tried a #morningroutine. My invitation to you is to have a play with different ways to start your day and make a note of what feels good for you.

Chapter 9

How to switch off

In case you didn't already know this: your 'to do' list is never going to end. There will always be something to add to it or you'll have to carry over to tomorrow that thing you ran out of time to finish, or an unexpected task comes in and derails everything. You'll never stop getting emails, messages and phone calls. This is just how the modern working world operates and there's no point fighting it by trying to achieve Inbox Zero or complete Asana. When you're overwhelmed by your workload it can paralyse you into inaction, further adding to the feeling of being behind. This can create a vicious cycle of trying to do everything, feeling overwhelmed and then not being as productive as you'd like. To help you combat the frustration and stress that can accompany managing your workload, I have some techniques you can test out to see if they help you to lessen the mental strain of the never-ending 'to do' list, just like they've helped me.

If you enjoy a list and you find it satisfying to tick things off, you'll like this first method of prioritising your day. Instead of creating a 'to do' list that has everything on it that you *want* to get done in a day, write out only the tasks that you *must* get done to be able to switch off your laptop and call it a day.

Here are the rules for creating a 'Done for the Day' list:

1. Look at how many hours you have available to work that day
2. For everything on your 'to do' list, estimate how much time you will need to complete the task
3. Choose the one task you must get done that day
4. Check you have enough time to do the task
5. If you have capacity to work on, or complete, the number one task then it goes on the list
6. Prioritise your remaining tasks in order of importance (check in with any deadlines)
7. For the remaining time you have available to you after scheduling in the number one task,

fit in your other tasks only if you have time to work on or complete them.

This list will likely be very short. Much shorter than your average daily 'to do' list. This is perfect because you've set a realistic goal for your workload instead of setting yourself up for stress and failure. Once you've hopefully completed your 'Done for the day' list, you can switch off your laptop with more peace of mind than on your incomplete 'to do' list days.

In the event of not completing your 'Done for the day' list, you can bump tasks to the next day once you've estimated how much time they will take to complete and how much time you have available to you. If you keep ending the day with items still on your daily list, learn from this and make the list shorter. If you've never estimated how long tasks will take you to complete, doing so start to build up better awareness of your capacity and manage your workload and time much more realistically.

The big benefit of sticking to a 'Done for the day' list is once you've ticked off your final task, your mind can relax. The problem we have with unfinished tasks is that we create a mental loop where we remind ourselves over and over to do the task. It's sitting there unfinished and your brain can't file it away until you've either completed it or assigned it to another day. A 'Done for the day' list is one of the key methods I've implemented that helps me to switch off at the end of the day. I've added the process of closing the open loops in my brain by always allocating time and space for unfinished tasks. You can also write down any ideas, or tasks that pop into your mind as they come up and assign time and space to think about them or action in the future. This helps to stop the inner running commentary we have of "I must remember to reply to John's email, then I need to send that PDF over to Sarah and I mustn't forget to order more printer ink tomorrow...". Put the tasks onto a list or into a tool like Asana or Trello, assign a date to them where you'll action it and let it out of your brain so you can have some downtime. And breathe!

How to turn off your laptop

To allow yourself to let go and enjoy your non-work time and be fully present with the folks around you without unfinished business looming over you, you need a hard stop after work. I've noticed a difference in how relaxed I feel in non-work time when I've merely closed my laptop versus actively shutting it down before I close it. I have a MacBook Air and it fires up so quickly when I open it up that if I leave it switched on but just closed, I can whip it open and fire off an email, check Asana or do a quick work task. This is dangerous in terms of relaxation time because if I know the laptop is still 'on', I don't feel I've actually finished working for the day.

If you also suffer from the feeling of always being 'on' for work, you can create a mini ritual for shutting down your laptop. Once you've completed your 'Done for the day' list or allocated any unfinished tasks to another day, go through the process of closing all your open browser tabs and applications and hit the Shut Down command. As the screen goes black and you close your laptop, state out loud: "I'm done for the day. I've finished working now." Put your laptop out of sight and pay attention to how you feel once you've made the commitment out loud that work is done. You can also do a few rounds of Box Breathing here to ground yourself after a busy day and move your energy into the space of free time, or gear yourself up for the school run, or whatever comes next for you!

Your work space

The exciting thing about entrepreneurship in the times we live in is that many of us can start a business from our kitchen table if we can get on the internet there. This is precisely what I did in January 2020. In our house we don't have an office room, so I would work from the dining table in the kitchen every day. I had to upgrade my broadband to the top speed as I quickly found it couldn't keep up with uploading and downloading files, and that was it! I was online and ready to earn some money from the comfort of my own home. When I left my marketing manager job to go all in on my business, I obviously didn't know that just over three months later we would all be locked down in our homes thanks to the pandemic. I think that intense scenario sped up how tired and disenchanted I was to become with working from home. In the spring of 2021 I was one year into running Cheer Up Marketing from my kitchen table and I was over it. I started to look for an office space away from my home. I wouldn't go as far as to say I missed my old commute, but I definitely missed the physical separation between work and home.

I decided that for my own sanity I needed to get out of the house to work and although coffee shops had opened up again by that time, there was a limit as to how long I could make my Americano last. Anyway, I needed somewhere to keep all my work papers, pens and printer (that I never use, but hey ho!). I booked some appointments to look at co-working and office spaces. I didn't have much on my list of requirements other than being able to get there by car (I needed parking nearby) and fast internet. Upon visiting the co-working spaces, I realised that the hours I spent doing Zoom meetings would make me a pretty antisocial co-worker and that environment wasn't going to work for me.

I had one option left: hire a room in an office building. I went to check out a converted lace factory six minutes drive from my home as the owner hired out individual rooms. I don't know if this was his sales tactic but he showed me the cheap room on the ground floor, north side of the building first, it was just not my vibe. It was dark and gloomy and I would rather have stayed at my kitchen table. Next, he took me up two flights of stairs and over to the south side of the building. As he opened the door to the more expensive option, I knew I had found my room. It was bright, airy and had a fantastic view over Nottingham. I could see the city, trees and Green's Windmill. I loved it and signed up on the spot. It was a commitment for a year and although I said it was the more expensive room, it was still an excellent deal and he assured me the internet access was good.

I moved in with the help of Adam (who carried everything up the two flights of stairs as there was no lift) and I've never looked back. Having a short drive to and from my office has made the world of difference to my mental approach to work. I do still work from the kitchen table on some days but it's now a choice rather than my only option. Having all my work stuff locked away in a dedicated space has helped me to switch off better at home.

If you are currently working from home and don't have a dedicated work space there, it's worth looking at hiring a desk or even an entire room like I did. When I'm at my office there's no dishwasher staring me in the face needing to be emptied. The Amazon man knocking on the door can't interrupt me. I don't waste time by "just popping a load in the washing machine". I'm at work in my office and I'm focussed on the task at hand. Adam helped me haul our old sofa up the stairs to my room, so now I have the option to work at a desk or sofa. And of course, I use the sofa for my meditation breaks!

The shift in my mindset that has come with having my own office space has also helped me to create more success in my business. When I was working at the kitchen table I felt a little bit like I was playing small. As soon as I got the keys to my office it felt like a big level up. I had a proper space to work from and it felt incredible. I'm all in on the business and I have my own space from which to build my version of success.

I recommend taking a look at what options are available in your local area, you might be surprised to get something for a reasonable price or discover you love to co-work a couple of days a week. Shift your environment, shift your energy.

Chapter 10

Making sleep your non-negotiable

As we've been looking at the physical space where we work and how to fully switch off at the end of the working day, it would be remiss of me not to cover working from bed. In short, it's not recommended. I know it's comfy because I've done it myself. In fact, some of this book was written from my bed! But working from bed is not conducive to a restful night's sleep and if there's one thing you need to be productive at work, it's rest. Writing this book was a big job and at points I got tired of sitting upright at my desk, kitchen table, Costa or sofa. I've been writing all over the place and sometimes I felt physically tired and craved writing in a semi-horizontal position with a fluffy white pillow as a desk. So I wrote a few chapters from my bed. I'm not perfect. BUT I do draw the line at doing client work from bed. An absolute hard no for me.

My bed is my sanctuary and your bed should be your sanctuary. A safe place to retreat and restore your body and mind. You can't fully relax if the place you go to is also the scene of your email duel with that difficult client. Or the place where you struggled to meet a deadline. Don't taint your bed with work drama because it'll be lingering there when you turn off the light at bedtime. Even if you enjoy your work most of the time, you still don't want to equate being in bed with being in work mode.

Why you need sleep

Being Positively Productive is about setting yourself up for success and to enjoy the journey. It's really hard to do this if you aren't getting enough sleep. You've probably heard that we need eight hours of sleep every night to function at our best, but this figure does vary for individuals.

A sleep survey carried out in the UK in 2022 by Chemist4U found that the average UK resident fails to achieve the recommended eight hours of sleep per night.

- The survey found that the average adult in the UK sleeps for just six hours and ten minutes per night
- The most sleep-deprived age group is 35-44 year olds who average 5.81 hours of sleep per night, or 2.19 hours less than the recommended eight

[See: www.chemist-4-u.com/guides/advice/insomnia/sleep-study/]

If you're getting less than the recommended eight hours of sleep at night, you're not alone, but this doesn't make it acceptable for you. I'm here to champion the benefits of extending how much sleep you're getting because the time you spend sleeping has a direct impact on your business success, health and overall happiness. Prioritising sleep is a non-negotiable in order to experience an uplift in success across all areas of your work and life and you really can't afford to settle for not getting enough sleep, or poor quality sleep.

With this in mind, you might have a good awareness of how much sleep you personally need to feel refreshed and 'on it' the next day. This is a useful insight because when you know how much sleep you need, you can take the necessary steps to make sure you get it as often as you can; every night if possible.

If you're curious about your biological programming when it comes to sleep, take the Sleep Chronotype Quiz over at:

https://thesleepdoctor.com/sleep-quizzes/chronotype-quiz/

Are you a Dolphin, Lion, Bear or Wolf?

The impact of not getting enough sleep

Aside from feeling foggy-headed and probably irritable when you don't get enough sleep, both the short-term and longer-term impact of not getting enough sleep makes for a sober read.

In the first instance you may suffer from:

- Lack of ability to focus
- Low motivation
- Forgetfulness
- Being more reactive
- Low mood
- Stress

Over time, a lack of sleep gives you an increased risk of:

- Obesity
- Cardiovascular disease
- Worsened depression and anxiety
- Reduced immune system functioning
- Diabetes
- Respiratory problems

The research into sleep and its effects on our bodies when we don't get enough of it is screaming at us to make bedtime a priority. In recent years there's been a real shift away from the entrepreneurial hustle culture of old; with trail blazers like Arianna Huffington sharing her shocking story of collapsing from exhaustion in 2007 and her subsequent championing of restoration and sleep for success.

I'm glad to see the back of this idea that to make headway in your business, you need to pull all-nighters or be a member of the 5 a.m. club. Five a.m. might be a great time for you to rise if you're going to bed early enough to get your full quota of sleep. The Sleep Chronotype quiz above will shed some light on when you should be going to bed and the optimal time of day for you to rise and work.

I'm fully on board with the anti-hustle movement and this book is my small contribution to that message. It's part of my mission and purpose to achieve success on my terms and share with others how they can do this too.

In this chapter, I'll give you some ideas for an evening ritual that will help you to sleep well and consequently wake up feeling ready to work productively and enjoy your day. Getting enough sleep is essential for you to thrive in life and business.

Your ideal bedtime ritual

There's an obvious place to start with getting a good night's sleep and it comes back to setting more boundaries with our old friend, the smartphone. There have been many studies on the effects of screen time on our ability to fall asleep at night. A quick Google will give you all the data you need so I won't give you all the statistics here but instead will invite you to reflect on how your evening phone usage might be affecting your sleep quality.

Phone hygiene tips for bedtime:

1. Don't check your email because you'll likely end up with a task that will open a loop in your brain that will repeat until you've dealt with the task. Starting this loop at bedtime is a bad idea. Leave emails until after breakfast (or lunch, ideally).
2. Don't check Social Media because you're never sure what you're going to see. Even if you've curated a feed full of lovely people and your Social Media experience is largely positive, you still don't need to see that your friend has lost their dog or read that Facebook group thread about the problem with local vandals. You can never guarantee that you won't read something that will affect you in an emotional way. Bedtime is not the time to risk reading something that will set you off.
3. Don't jump into the WhatsApp thread. Because once you reply, you'll get more replies and then you feel obligated to see the conversation through to the end which can take precious time away from your sleep. The chat can also open more loops of things you need to do or remember in your brain. You

don't need to act on this at night time. Leave it until tomorrow.

4. Don't look at your calendar for the next day. Ideally you will know what you're up to because you'll have shuffled things around after completing your 'Done for the day' list earlier. Checking your calendar before you go to sleep will have you mentally preparing for the day ahead when your mind should be relaxing. I've found I can spend all night working in my sleep if I think too much about the following day.

If, like me, you find the pull of the iPhone too compelling sometimes, I'll remind you of my top tip for creating a strong boundary with your phone - put it out of reach. There are boxes you can buy to lock your phone in but I've found the car boot is super effective because it involves going outside to retrieve the phone.

Bedtime wind down strategies as an alternative to scrolling

If your current bedtime routine involves a thorough scroll before you try to go to sleep, it's worth referring back to your Positivity Boosters to identify something else relaxing you can do instead.

Here are some of my favourite pre-bed alternatives to scrolling:

- Take a bath! *No phones allowed. Read a book or magazine instead, or use this as your quiet time for the day and be alone with your thoughts.*
- Read a book. *Kindles are allowed and there are some interesting studies which show that pre-bed screen time from a Kindle doesn't have the same negative effect on our sleep as phone screen time.*
- Listen to a meditation or sleep story. *You might need your phone to access your favourite meditation app or recording which can make this one a little risky. I've found a way around this by using my iPad for streaming meditations as I'm not habitually trained to use my iPad for scrolling.*
- Practice mindfulness. *No phone required; just focus on your breathing and awareness of your body's contact with the bed, pillow and covers.*

If you watch TV in bed then it's worth noting what this does to your sleep quality versus the nights when you don't watch it. I'm so committed to having the best sleep ever that we don't have a TV in our bedroom. Watching TV in our house is confined to the living room as a family or as a couple and we don't scroll or have laptops out while we're watching (we leave our devices in a different room or mine is in the car boot!). I actually don't like TV very much because I often can't shake the feeling there's a better way I could be spending my time but I can appreciate that for the telly lovers out there, this one might feel like giving up a favourite late night activity. All I'm inviting you to do is test out nights where you don't watch TV in bed immediately before trying to fall asleep and noting how much time you end up sleeping for and how rested you feel in the morning.

Creating your new favourite bedtime ritual

I'm aware I've given you a list of things not to do at bedtime which might be things you enjoy and currently do to unwind (watching TV and scrolling your phone). Rather than making it feel like a chore to implement a strict routine to get great sleep, I want this process to feel like a treat for you every night.

This is where creating your own personal bedtime ritual comes into play.

The aims are your bedtime ritual should be:

- To calm a busy mind
- To relax your body
- To reduce your stress levels
- To make you feel happy and experience gratitude
- To help you fall asleep within ten to twenty minutes

An example bedtime ritual

Here I'll share my ritual which has been the same for three years now and I can confirm I fall asleep within twenty minutes; I sleep through the night and I wake up feeling fully rested and restored. There are exceptions to this over the past three years as Penny has grown from three years old to six years old and we've had phases of illness (catching vomit in my dressing gown was one memorable occasion), night wakes, early morning rising and a particularly rough period of nightmares thanks to an episode of Barbie on Netflix (rated U, I might add) where Penny became terrified of the idea of a "spooky box". That damn box resulted in her coming into our bed because she was so scared I couldn't reassure her enough for her to go back to sleep in her own room.

Even when we've had disrupted sleep as a family I recover quickly because, crucially, I wasn't overtired to start with. I've had nights of broken sleep where I've still felt fine the next day and have been productive at work because my sleep routine is so strong that I very rarely feel under rested. I want this for you as it's inevitable, even without kids, that at some point we will have rough nights or broken sleep. I want to equip you so that when poor sleep happens, you aren't broken.

My bedtime ritual

Here's what I've been doing every night at home, or away, for at least three years now. This includes when on holiday and even when camping in a tent! I'm never without my bedtime journal and a pen.

Step 1: No phone screen time after 9pm (ninety minutes before sleep)

Step 2: Skincare routine (cleanse, tone, moisturise)

Optional step 2.5: An evening shower turning to cold for last two minutes

Step 3: Get into bed and write down three wins from the day and three things I'm grateful for. Write down anything else that's come up today or I feel I need to get down onto paper.

Step 4: Read my book for twenty to thirty minutes

Step 5: (Latest 10.30 p.m.) Switch bedside lamp to Sunset mode

Step 6: Pop in Airpods and listen to a sleep meditation

Step 7: Fall asleep!

I wake at 7 a.m. (ish) which means this routine gives me at least eight hours of sleep. Some days I rise earlier to do my chosen morning 'me time' activity. If I'm rising at 6 a.m., I'll be sure to be switching my bedside lamp to sunset mode around 10 p.m. and plugging into the meditation a little earlier than on the days I rise later. If you're interested, I came up as a Bear in the Sleep Chronotype quiz and sleeping between 10 p.m. and 7 a.m. is my sweet spot to feel rested.

Based on how many hours sleep you need, and if you're not sure, start with the recommended eight hours then work backwards from your required wake time and start your bedtime ritual in plenty of time so that you can allow around twenty minutes to fall asleep.

Committing to taking the steps to secure more, better quality sleep is a non-negotiable for your success. You've picked up this book to find out more about how you can be more productive and sleep is a big part of that. Please don't settle for less sleep because you think it's too difficult to change your current bedtime habits. If you live with a partner or children, share your sleep goals with them. My daughter enjoys her bedtime routine of dim lights, stories and loves the scent of a sleepy essential oil she applies to pulse points before snuggling down. She likes white noise to fall asleep to; her current favourite is a track on the Calm app called Milky Way Soundscape.

Adam has also become committed to better sleep. I joke all the time that when I met him he was this tattooed, rock 'n' roll guy driving a pick-up truck and we were up late partying all the time. These days he's there in bed early with his sunset lamp, Tempur support pillow, eye mask on and plugged into a calm sleep story. I will say, he looks great for forty.

Science-based tips for improving sleep quality

Now that we've sorted your new bedtime ritual, hopefully you're excited to go to bed tonight and wake up feeling like you can take on anything because you're so well rested. Let's now look at some research-backed tips and tricks you can add in to build on the basics of sleep hygiene and a bedtime ritual.

1. Be consistent

Your body likes routine when it comes to sleep. Sticking to your routine by going to bed at roughly the same time each night and waking at the same time will help you to fall asleep easily and enjoy good quality sleep. *See research by Matthew Walker PhD for more information on this.*

2. Set your body clock

Your Circadian rhythms are influenced by daylight, exercise, meals and sleep at a certain time. You can influence your internal body clock by getting sunlight into your eyes in the morning. I walk the school run to achieve this or sit outside with my morning cuppa in the warm weather.

You can invest in a sunrise lamp to help you rise using bright light instead of the shock of a noisy alarm. In our house we each have a Lumie Bodyclock on our bedside tables. I double up with my audio alarm on the other side of the room so I have to get up to turn it off but I'm already awake thanks to the light filtering through my eyelids. It's a much gentler way to wake up.

Watch when you exercise because thrashing it out at the gym in the evening will produce cortisol and as a stress hormone, this may negatively affect your sleep. Another reason to get your gym time in during the day while all the 9-5ers are at work!

3. Check your caffeine intake

I know if I drink caffeine after 6 p.m., I struggle to have a restful night's sleep. Be aware of your caffeine consumption and if you've never tried it, switch to decaf in the afternoon or evenings. Note how you feel this affects your sleep quality.

I read a study about the positive effects of swapping out that first caffeinated drink of the day for decaf.

Caffeine temporarily blocks the signal from adenosine, a sleep chemical in the brain. Adenosine continues to build up and then eventually breaks through, causing a dramatic crash, often mid-afternoon if you've had a morning coffee or tea. About nine months ago now, Adam and I swapped our morning Yorkshire Tea for the decaf version and we both feel that we've skipped the 3 p.m. slump as a result. We now wait the recommended ninety minutes after waking before having caffeine. Worth testing for yourself if you drink caffeine first thing and find you crash in the afternoons or need to keep topping up with more caffeine to keep going.

4. No booze before bed

Alcohol might make you feel relaxed and sleepy but it stops you from having REM sleep - the deep sleep required for your brain to restore. Drinking a lot can also impair your breathing at night and isn't good for staying asleep.

I've never been a big drinker at home but I've become even more sober-focussed recently and I've swapped my Friday night craft beer for a fancy tonic and a slice (no gin).

. . .

5. Choose light meals if eating late

Eating big meals too close to bedtime will affect your sleep quality. I used to struggle with timing dinner as I often waited until after Penny had gone to bed to eat dinner with Adam. She eats her dinner at around 5 p.m. which is too early for me as with a 10 p.m. bedtime, I'm starving again by then! I'd prefer to eat at seven which is too late for her. We haven't perfected our evening meal routine yet but I'm testing eating at around six and having a light dessert-style snack at around eight so my stomach doesn't start rumbling in bed. I've also increased my protein intake which is helping me to feel fuller for longer and reduces my craving to dunk half a packet of chocolate Hobnobs in my decaf cuppa at nine.

6. Try magnesium

Adam swears by his post-dinner magnesium drink for falling asleep quickly. I told you he's rock 'n' roll. There have been limited yet encouraging studies showing that magnesium supplements may improve sleep quality and duration.

7. Enjoy essential oils

There are some gorgeous smelling blends of essential oils you can buy that aid with sleep. I love Neom's Perfect Night's Sleep blend which I also have as a hand cream and pillow mist. Try pulse point oils, scented candles or diffusers to make your bedroom smell like a spa paradise.

8. Keep a notepad by your bed

I've shared my journaling practice which helps me to release any thoughts and sleep peacefully. If you find you often have ideas, worries or things 'to do' that pop into your head at bedtime then keep a pen and paper by the bed to write them down so you can close the loop and relax knowing that you can deal with it tomorrow.

I've intentionally gone into a lot of detail about sleep because it's one of the biggest factors involved with how productive you are and how happy and healthy you feel. We are all more resilient to challenges when we're well-rested and as business owners we have to face challenges over and over. To aid you in adopting a growth mindset for success, make sure you implement changes to your sleep to get you as close to eight hours a night as possible.

Conclusion: Being Positively Productive for life

I hope you've taken away some practical ideas for becoming more productive in your work but even more importantly, as you've gone through each chapter, you've taken some time to pause and reflect on what you're doing in your business and that you've gained some clarity on your Big Why.

If I've convinced you to start prioritising your wellness, happiness and the things that matter the most to you in life more than you were doing before you read this book then I've achieved my goal! I can't stress enough how much my business changed for the better when I took the time to work on myself and my mindset and committed to make incremental changes to feel more positive every day. I really want as many business owners as possible to understand the Power of Positivity in terms of achieving success. Please share this book with someone you think could do with a positivity boost, or would benefit from some of the strategies around managing time and building a business.

Keep this book by your workspace as a reminder to slow down, take a breath, implement the tips and tricks I share within it to reduce overwhelm and come back brighter when challenges threaten to knock you off course.

You've got this!

Kelly :)

Acknowledgments

Thank you to my husband, Adam, who did more than his fair share of bedtimes and often ate dinner alone while I finished writing this book. Without his encouragement and support, I wouldn't have taken the leap to start my own business in the first place. He's the best!

About the Author

Kelly Cookson is a marketing strategist, copywriter and certified Positive Psychology Coach who has grown her online business to a six figure annual turnover working just twenty hours a week.

Kelly has over fifteen years of experience in digital marketing and a first-class honours degree in Business Information Management. She has been featured in the press, including Medium and The Daily Express, and has been interviewed live on GB News about how she has built a successful business alongside being a parent.

After having her daughter in 2017 and spending a couple of years working part-time, Kelly wanted more flexibility in her working life. With no savings and a second-hand laptop, she made the leap into self-employment and started building her online marketing business from her kitchen table.

With the newfound freedom her business has given her, Kelly enjoys hanging out with her daughter, friends and family and can be found in the sauna dreaming up her next big thing! She is currently learning to play electric guitar and is writing a non-fiction book to help more entrepreneurs market their businesses more efficiently.

Kelly is passionate about mixing smart marketing strategy with a strong mindset to support her clients to supercharge their business success.

The best way to keep up with Kelly's work is by subscribing to her email list over at www.cheerupmarketing.com

---

Connect with me

www.cheerupmarketing.com

facebook.com/kelly.cookson.5

instagram.com/cheerupmarketing

linkedin.com/in/kcookson

Printed in Great Britain
by Amazon

31866064R00116